How to Set-up and Run Your Prosperous Astrology Business

A Guide for Aspiring Astrologers

Alison Price

HOW TO SET UP AND RUN YOUR ASTROLOGY BUSINESS – A guide for aspiring astrologers

© 2018 Alison Price – All rights reserved

Published by Starzology Media

All rights reserved. No part of this book may be reproduced in any form or by any electronic or mechanical means, including information storage and retrieval systems, without permission in writing from the publisher, with the exception of reviewers who are quoting brief passages.

ISBN 978-1-976752-568

Revised edition

To Tim

Table of Contents

INTRODUCTION 10

HOW TO KNOW WHEN TO GO PRO 12
   THE 5 LEVELS OF ASTROLOGER 13
   WHEN TO GO PRO 16
   PLANNING A TWO YEAR WINDOW WITH MARS 18
   YOUR INTERNAL DIALOGUE 21
   CONSULTATION AND CHART READING REVIEW.......................23
   CHART INDICATORS FOR AN ASTROLOGER 24
   WHAT TYPE OF ASTROLOGER YOU ARE 26
   YOUR URANUS SIGN...27
   YOUR URANUS HOUSE 30
   YOUR URANUS ASPECTS 32
   YOUR URANUS DIRECTION 34

GETTING STARTED 35
   YOU AND YOUR SUN 36
   YOUR NAME AS GIVEN 39
   YOUR MIDHEAVEN - YOUR BUSINESS 41
   HOW TO SELECT YOUR BUSINESS NAME 43
   YOUR TAG LINE 44
   YOUR DOMAIN NAME 45
   YOUR WEBSITE 48
   ON DAY ONE OF THE LIFE OF YOUR WEBSITE 52
   IN WEEK ONE OF THE LIFE OF YOUR WEBSITE 54
   IN MONTH ONE OF THE LIFE OF YOUR WEBSITE 55
   DO THESE OTHER ACTIVITIES 56
   YOUR EMAIL ADDRESSES 58
   YOUR EMAIL SIGNATURE 60
   YOUR DESIGN 62
   YOUR BUSINESS CARD 64
   YOUR BRAND 65
   YOUR PLATFORM..66
   YOUR BIOGRAPHY 69

YOUR PROMOTIONAL PHOTO 71
YOUR PHOTO LIBRARY 73
YOUR ONE PAGE INFORMATION SHEET 74
YOUR ELEVATOR PITCH 75
YOUR SOCIAL MEDIA PRESENCE 78
YOUR SOLAR FIRE COMPLIMENTS TEXT 80

HOW TO FIND CLIENTS 82
OWN YOUR NICHE 83
YOUR PRODUCTS AND SERVICES 86
HOW YOUR NATAL CHART ATTRACTS CLIENTS 88
HOW TO FIND CLIENTS 91
YOUR OUTER PLANET SIGNATURE 92
YOUR OUTER PLANET SIGNATURE 94
HOW TO TAKE A BOOKING 98

MONEY 102
THE FOUR MONEY HOUSES 103
THE PART OF FORTUNE 105
THE CONDITION OF THE PART OF FORTUNE AS REGARDS MONEY 106
THE PART OF FORTUNE IN THE HOUSES 108
HOW TO SET FEES 110
WHAT TO CHARGE FOR A ONE HOUR ASTROLOGICAL CONSULTATION
....111
HOW TO HANDLE REQUESTS FOR FREE READINGS 113
OFFERING DISCOUNTS 115
WHEN TO QUIT YOUR DAY JOB 118
YOUR OFFICE SPACE AND WORKING HOURS 120
YOUR ASSETS AND LIABILITIES 122
THINGS THAT SEEM LIKE ASSETS BUT ARE REALLY LIABILITIES 124

DAILY TIME CHALLENGES 125
YOUR PRODUCTIVE PREPARATION TIME 126
A DAY IN THE LIFE OF AN ASTROLOGER 127
7 DAYS TO A BETTER CHART READING 129
10 THINGS TO DO BEFORE YOUR CLIENT ARRIVES 134
5 THINGS TO DO AFTER YOUR CLIENT LEAVES 137

10 Classic Comments Clients Make 139
How to Give an Astrological Referral 143

YOUR PROFESSIONAL IMPROVEMENT 146

Your Annual Astrology Review 148
Peer Review – Is It For You? 150
Be Yourself and Be Your Sun 153
A Successful Astrologer 155
Your Comfort Zone 157
What Type of Astrologer are You? 160
Your Creative Writing Time 162
Astrological Certification, Yes or No? 164
How to Become a Certified Astrologer 166

YOUR PLACE IN THE ASTROLOGICAL COMMUNITY 167

How to Create an Astrology Study Group 168
Astrology Software 171
Add Twelve Hours and Reverse the Signs 173
How to Have Fun at an Astrology Conference 174
Your Relationship With Other Astrologers 180
Support Local Astrology 182
Glossary of Astrological Terms 185
Short Form Codes 189
Default Aspect Orbs 191
Recommended Reading and Software 192

MORE FOR YOU 195

About the Author 196
Other Books by Alison Price 197

Introduction

How to Set Up and Run Your Astrology Business is a guide for astrologers who want to start their business and move from amateur to professional status.

A professional astrologer will accept payment for a reading whereas an amateur astrologer does not. The difference is a little thing called money. Once you get over the fear of failure paralysis and embrace the possibility of creating a career in astrology (and we all can) you move into another phase and then pose the question "Where to now?" This is where this book comes into play as it shows you how to organize your life, to make room for astrology and to include the creative process. This book is for people who know how to do astrology. There are seven main sections:

1. How to know when to go professional – read your chart to find an auspicious time.

2. Getting started – some planning and micro-business basics.

3. How to find clients – that your clients are attracted to your chart.

4. Money – pricing your services, earning and your approach to money.

5. Your professional improvement – and how to be aware and improve your astrology practice.

6. Daily time challenges – managing the day-to-day business and clients

7. Your place in the astrological community – "it takes a village" and how to support others.

There are sections on platform building which is the most important mental shift that the budding astrologer can make and dealing with clients by creating boundaries between yourself and your client. There is information on setting fees and payment methods and tips on monitoring your own progress. Throughout the book there are several Aspiring Astrologer Activities, and these are for your own personal pleasure.

How to Know When to Go Pro

Amateur versus Professional Astrologer

To go pro, means to become a professional. The difference between an amateur and a professional is that amateurs do not get paid but professionals do get paid.

To change your status as an astrologer from amateur to professional is a huge step and requires adjustment on many levels and particularly mental, financial, psychological and physical levels.

This chapter explores what is required to go pro and how you can reach this status in your astrological career.

The Path to Becoming an Astrologer

Your personal astrological development can take years. You may remain at one stage or level for decades and this happens when life gets in the way. Many people start astrology as adults and may have a day job and other commitments that demand their time and energy. You can always pick up where you left off and continue your journey towards astrology. The process of becoming an astrologer includes particular milestones. Some are based on your knowledge of astrology some are mental states that change, and others are professional decision you make. I am not saying that aspiring to become master astrologer is everyone's goal, but the process of becoming an astrologer is clear.

The 5 Levels of Astrologer

There are five levels of astrologer and different criteria or milestones to be reached at each stage of the astrologer's evolution. Consider where you are today as you start this journey and check back in six and twelve months' time to see how far you have come.

Level 1: Hobbyist astrologer

- You read your horoscope every week
- You know your own and your family member's Sun signs
- You can discuss astrology at a dinner party
- You know enough to be dangerous (ha ha)

Level 2: Student astrologer – (All of the above plus)

- You have attended an astrology lecture
- You own five astrology books including an ephemeris
- You subscribe to The Mountain Astrologer
- You have taken at least one astrology lesson
- You are considering attending a conference
- You own Astro Gold

Level 3: Amateur astrologer – (All of the above plus)

- You can read the glyphs in a chart
- You know the signs, planets, houses and aspects
- You own ten astrology books including a Table of Houses
- You have at least one planet specific book

- You are a member of your local astrology group
- You have taken a formal astrology education course
- You can interpret charts for family and friends
- You can debate houses systems
- You have attended an astrology conference
- You own the latest version of Solar Fire
- You know at least four forecasting techniques
- You are invited to speak locally

Level 4: Professional astrologer – (All the above plus)

- You can construct a chart from scratch (without a computer)
- You can calculate forecasts from scratch (without a computer)
- You have an extensive astrology library with duplicate editions
- You subscribe to all the trade periodicals
- You are a member of the international astrology associations
- You accept payments for your work
- Your income surpasses US$12000 a year from astrology
- You are invited to speak internationally
- You have appeared on TV or radio
- You write a column/blog
- You own your astrology website
- You have published an astrology book

Level 5: Master astrologer – (All the above plus)

- You have been a professional (accepts payments) for at least ten years
- You are considered a guru in the astrological community
- You have written more than one book
- Your income exceeds US$60000 a year from astrology
- Your name is known by the general public
- You are the Keynote speaker
- You are a recipient of astrology awards acknowledging your contribution
- You may have forsaken daily consultations for focused research
- You are the Astrorati of the day

Aspiring Astrologer Activity

What level are you at today?

Which level will you be in two years' time?

At which level will you be satisfied?

When to Go Pro

An astrology business usually blossoms when your natal Uranus (astrology) and your Midheaven (going public with a business) are stimulated this happens usually by transit, secondary progression or other forecast technique contact.

It cajust be on the day you finally 'get' astrology, which usually occurs at a transit or progressed contact. If you know the exact day your life changed and started your astrological awakening write it down in your notebook. You can answer the following questions and gather the information in your notebook.

Your Uranus Transits

The years when transiting Uranus makes an exact Ptolemaic aspect to your Midheaven are important, but if you can get the dates of the transits three passes, that is very good.

- When does transiting Uranus conjunct your Midheaven?
- When does transiting Uranus sextile your Midheaven?
- When does transiting Uranus square your Midheaven?
- When does transiting Uranus trine your Midheaven?
- When transiting Uranus conjoins two other points and planet in your chart it is a good indicator for starting to go pro.
- When does transiting Uranus conjunct your Midheaven ruler?
- When does transiting Uranus conjunct your natal Saturn?

Your Solar Return Chart

The year when your solar return Sun falls in the 10th or 6th house of your solar return chart.

- Which year is your solar return Sun in the 6th house?
- Which year is your solar return Sun in the 10th house?

Your Secondary Progressions

The years when your secondary progressed Moon conjoins your natal Midheaven and passes through your tenth house are good indicators for starting to go pro.

- Progressed Moon conjunct natal Midheaven
- Your progressed New Moon (previous)
- Your progressed New Moon (next)
- When does your secondary progressed Uranus station direct?

Your Solar Arc Directions

In solar arc directions the year when your natal Uranus is stimulated by a conjunction from any of; the solar arc Sun, Mars, Jupiter, Midheaven, Ascendant or Midheaven ruler suggest a growing interest in going pro with astrology.

Find the dates when the following occur:

- Solar arc directed Sun conjunct your natal Uranus
- Solar arc directed Mars conjunct your natal Uranus
- Solar arc directed Jupiter conjunct your natal Uranus
- Solar arc directed Midheaven conjunct your natal Uranus
- Solar arc directed Ascendant conjunct your natal Uranus
- Solar arc directed Midheaven ruler conjunct natal Uranus

Planning a Two-Year Window with Mars

Mars is the planet of beginnings, pioneering action, expended effort and it shows where you are happy to burn energy. Mars rules the sign Aries the Ram, which it the first sign of the tropical zodiac, and is the traditional ruler of Scorpio the Scorpion. As the first planet further from the Sun than the Earth, Mars takes about two years to make one complete pass through the zodiac. Because of this orbital period Mars can be used to kick start events and courses of action in your life.

Transiting Mars - Timing is Everything

Having two years to do something may seem a long stretch but if you plan to start a micro-business it can offer a convenient time span. The trick is to begin what you want to do when Mars transits the planet in your chart that rules the activity you want to start.

- When Mars contacts your Sun, Moon, Uranus, Ascendant or Midheaven directly it may be time.
- Mars conjoining your natal Sun is good for doing what you want and getting to the heart of the matter.
- As Mars approaches your natal Moon it suggests active, and not reactive, behavior and you can use this emotionally charged time appropriately for taking the plunge.
- When Mars nears radix Uranus it can create a spark for astrology and this may be the ideal time to overcome inertia if you have been thinking about an astrology business but not actually done anything about it – yet.
- If Mars crosses your birth ascendant your personality gets fired up and you display confidence.
- The red planet crossing your Midheaven indicates it is time to act on your career by taking a stab at competing for the career you want and being in the competition for the glory.

Close Encounters of the Third Kind

If you are lucky enough to receive a Martian three contact transit (direct, retrograde, direct) to an important natal planet or your Ascendant or Midheaven, it shows the time is ripe to expend the effort required to get that particular project started. Sometimes a Mars transit passes by quietly. If you look ahead and get the important dates in the next two years it can show the best time to launch your astrology career.

Mars Three Pass Transit

At the first direct transit you may initially be enamored by the idea and inspired.

During the retrograde pass doubt can set in about the validity of the venture.

Finally, on the last contact your plans should be steaming along and well under way.

Aspiring Astrologer Activity

Find the date when transiting Mars…

Conjoins your Sun.

Conjoins your Moon.

Conjoins your Uranus.

Conjoins your Ascendant.

Conjoins your Midheaven.

Your Internal Dialogue

If you have been toying with the idea of starting your own astrology business but you have not done so yet, it may be because there are some thoughts running through your head that can hold you back. You may have you said one of these statements.

"It's just a hobby"

Hobbies are shown in your fifth and sixth houses. The fifth house hobbies and creative pursuits like pottery or making things, and the sixth house hobbies are yoga, hiking, serving others as a daily hobby or ritual. Often astrology does start as a hobby and for many it can remain so, but that you are reading this shows you want to make it more and start your business.

"I might get it wrong"

Reading astrology charts for others does open you up to making mistakes. We all make mistakes and most of us get things wrong now and then. You can grow in confident at reading astrology charts through a thorough astrological education and by practicing readings. Saturn is the planet that suggests our fears and awareness of our shortcomings. Your Saturn placement may have made you fear to strive for what you want. You can overcome Saturn fear by turning the tables on Saturn and using the strength of the planet through achieving certificates, honors and awards in astrology.

"What will the neighbors think?"

If you have third house planets you can be concerned with what the neighbors think. If Mercury is in the third house it can be a constant inner dialogue. The solution is to use third house planets and a tricky Mercury complex to educate yourself through astrology knowledge and understanding the two main resistance points for astrology from the general public. Resistance to astrology usually comes from two quarters - religion and science. The religious detractors will put the case that only God can predict so fortune telling is a sin, and the scientific resistance will usually be that astrologers use the tropical zodiac and scientists use the sidereal zodiac and that's why astrology is always wrong. These arguments can come to you in many forms, but the main thrusts are the same. To prepare for these two concerns from others you can write down your responses (religion and science) so you have some verbal defense when these objections come up. It is not your job to change others views but to respectfully be able to state your own. Usually you will get this resistance from outsiders but know that it often comes from your inner circle of family and friends. Learn how to tactfully deal with naysayers.

"I do not know everything"

Lack of astrological knowledge is probably the easiest obstacle to address. If you do not do not know enough about astrology take some classes, courses, workshops, master classes and conferences. Get yourself certified by a reputable astrology teaching institution (There is a list of excellent astrology teaching bodies in the appendix). Go where astrologers are and join your local astrology group where you can attend meeting and events.

"I'll never be good enough"

Here the issue is in your second house of self-esteem, self-worth and how you value yourself. If you have a lack of self-esteem and harbour beliefs that no longer serve you it can make you unconfident to practice astrology. If this sis your issue I suggest taking it slowly and monitor your progress. Read one chart at a time and take your time. But afterwards do a private client reading review and list where you felt you did good and where you could have improved. In this way you can look back in three months' time when you have read ten charts and see your improvement.

Consultation and Chart Reading Review

Each time you do a chart reading keep some records and write down the details. This is more important in the initial stages of your nosiness.

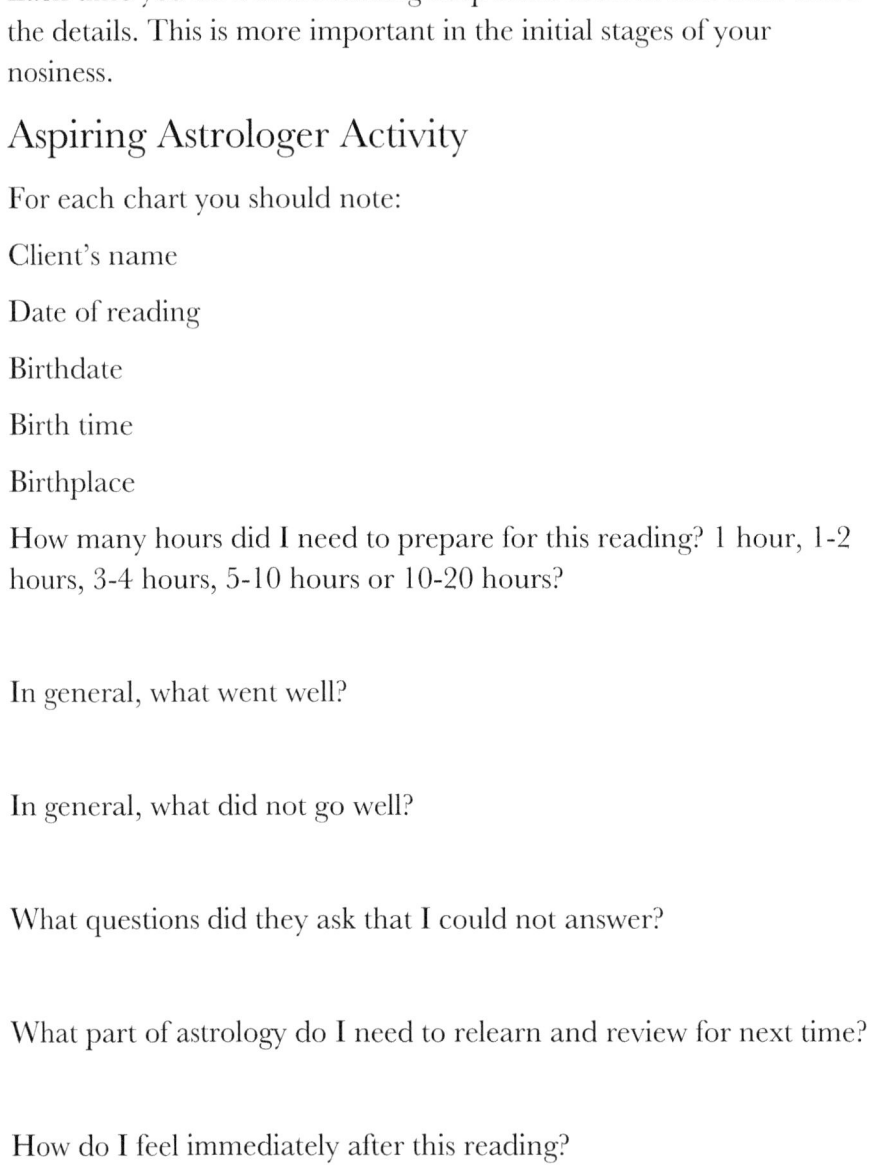

Aspiring Astrologer Activity

For each chart you should note:

Client's name

Date of reading

Birthdate

Birth time

Birthplace

How many hours did I need to prepare for this reading? 1 hour, 1-2 hours, 3-4 hours, 5-10 hours or 10-20 hours?

In general, what went well?

In general, what did not go well?

What questions did they ask that I could not answer?

What part of astrology do I need to relearn and review for next time?

How do I feel immediately after this reading?

Chart Indicators for an Astrologer

Your natal chart gives clues as to the type of astrologer you are likely to be. Modern astrologers take Uranus, as the ruler of our craft and the traditional ruler is Mercury.

During transits to sensitive planets and chart points in your natal chart external changes may occur to alter your life path. When you experience secondary progressions to sensitive planets and chart points is may be a time when internal changes are likely to develop to alter your karmic direction.

The above two points, of transits and secondary progressions to your natal chart, can suggest times in your life when astrology will begin to loom large. The more forecast triggers that happen at once, the more likely it will be.

Uranus

As the modern ruler of astrology and astrologers Uranus is a strong indicator for an astrologer if it is conjoined your ascendant, Sun, Midheaven or Mercury or, if Uranus is oriental where it suggests your vocation. There are many instances where Uranus aspects the oriental planet in well-known astrologer's charts. All natal aspects to your Uranus will modify the type of astrologer you are likely to become. Uranus conjunctions are the strongest indicators. When your natal Uranus is stimulated by progressions from the Sun, Mercury, Ascendant or Midheaven an interest in astrology will probably develop.

Mercury

The traditional ruler of astrology and astrologers is Mercury the planet of information gathering and dispersal and of scribing the events of the day. When your natal Mercury receives aspects from transiting Uranus astrology becomes an interest.

Jupiter

As the philosopher and teacher, Jupiter often conjoins, squares or opposes the Sun or Uranus in an astrologer's natal chart. It also frequently contacts Mercury, the Ascendant or Midheaven. When natal Jupiter is stimulated by transiting Uranus or progressed Mercury it may spark an interest and you will seek astrological knowledge

Aquarius

Aquarius on the first house cusp shows a personal interest in astrology. On the Midheaven the water bearer indicates that a business can be made from astrology. When your secondary progressed or solar arc directed ascendant or Midheaven enters Aquarius the focus of your life will shift. This change alone will not confirm astrology, but it will if supported by other indicators.

Many factors contribute to an interest in astrology. If you take your passion for astrology a step further, it makes sense to look at the career indicators for an astrologer in your chart. This can guide you towards fulfilling the potential shown by your natal placements. If you live in tune with your natal chart you are more likely to be satisfied with your life and you can more readily be the type of astrologer your chart suggests, rather than one which you think you should be, by attempting to emulate those around you.

What Type of Astrologer You Are

Your Natal Chart

The nature of your natal chart can suggest the type of astrologer you are. Again, we look at your natal Uranus and its condition to see how astrology can manifest in your life.

Your Uranus Complex

Your Uranus complex is all the information we can gather about Uranus in your chart. We look at Uranus' house, sign, direction, dipositor, house ruler, sign rulers and any other chart details.

Whether Uranus is the handle of a bucket, most elevated or oriental will show the prominence that Uranus has in your chart and thus how astrology has status in your life.

Aspiring Astrologer Activity – Uranus Complex

Note your Uranus' sign.

Note your Uranus' house.

List your Uranus aspects; conjunctions, sextiles, squares, trines, oppositions and quintiles.

Note your tightest Uranus aspect.

Note your Uranus direction; direct, stationary or retrograde.

Your Uranus Sign

Uranus spends around seven years in each zodiac sign in turn and it can be considered as a "generational" placement. Uranus by sign is not particularly useful in finding the message about your astrological direction.

Uranus in Aries

This sign above the others tends toward you being an astrological entrepreneur. Running a one man (or woman) show comes naturally and you can strike out on your own early on in your career.

Uranus in Taurus

With Uranus in Taurus you can move forward to create a body of work. This sign inclines towards making money with astrology either for yourself or your clients. You can attract wealthy clients.

Uranus in Gemini

When Uranus is in Gemini you will attend many astrology classes and workshops and can be the perpetual student. This sign for Uranus is inclined to do multiple astrology techniques at once. You may be constantly chopping and changing what you offer and how your run your business. Word of mouth will bring in the clients.

Uranus in Cancer

When Uranus is in Cancer it shows that you like a home based astrology business and you like to work on your family's charts all the time. Your clients will feel cared for and you will have a good client base most of the time.

Uranus in Leo

Uranus in Leo suggests you will do creative astrology. You are good working with children's and young people's charts. You can do birthday party astrology and make it fun for your clients. Uranus in Leo benefits from lots of astrology props, like terrestrial globes and wooden carved planet glyphs. This is a good placement for astro-drama and role-playing type consultations. This position indicates you will be good at risk astrology such as the stock market and day-trading astrology.

Uranus in Virgo

Uranus in Virgo supports critical astrology and the detailed analysis of charts which can lead to too much time being spent on chart preparation and an inability to actually read for others. The constant revisions and may cause hesitation in getting an astrology business going.

Uranus in Libra

If you have Uranus in Libra, you will do astrology best with a partner. Not necessarily a personal partner but a business partner as a team of two. You need someone to bounce ideas and reading interpretations off before going public. It may even be that you both do the consultations, alternating with being the receptionist and then the chart reader. Taking it in turns.

Uranus in Scorpio

With Uranus in Scorpio you want to know how astrology works and have the desire to interpret the lives of others and this is very good for an astrology business. Spend time preparing your business strategy and keep it low key to succeed. Discretion is everything for Uranus in Scorpio.

Uranus in Sagittarius

Astrologers with Uranus in Sagittarius can be well travelled and lecture around the world. If you belong to this group, you are good at spreading the message of astrology and teaching others how to develop a personal journey and life-path with your astrological insights.

Uranus in Capricorn

You can get a professional astrology business going as soon as you like. Do not get bogged down in the red tape of the business side but set it up properly. Start working towards a solid client base and watch your robust reputation bring clients to you. With this placement you can build a business that other astrologers aspire towards and want to emulate.

Uranus in Aquarius

Astrology for all is the way to go when Uranus is in its own sign. You will strive to provide astrological understanding for everyone and as such may not consult in the strictest meaning of the word. You are better in commune type settings by spreading the word to many.

Uranus in Pisces

There can be a delicate touch to your astrology business when Uranus is in Pisces. Here you want to make sure your client fully understands what you have said in your reading and you may spend too much time with each client to make it a viable business.

Your Uranus House

Your chart hints at where you can be an astrologer by the house placement of your Uranus. As an astrologer you may need to do many things (as all micro-business people have to), but the house that Uranus tenants suggests the strengths that you have for expressing astrology through your natal Uranus.

Uranus in the First House

This placement does incline towards someone who can say "I am an astrologer" and they may assert this early on in the career.

Uranus in the Second House

Uranus in the second house suggests that you can earn money from astrology and have an income from astrology.

Uranus in the Third House

This is good for astrology teachers. You can set up class structures, learning syllabi and even start an astrology school.

Uranus in the Fourth House

A classic sign for a home based astrologer at the kitchen table. Perhaps moving into the basement or simply having a home/office for your astrology will appeal.

Uranus in the Fifth House

This person is good at party astrology, either using astrology as pure entertainment as in "book me for your event" or in a Tupperware style "party" where friends get together for a fun afternoon or evening.

Uranus in the Sixth House

With this Uranus placement you can make astrology your job and you will spend time in the daily ritual that an astrology business entails. To keep records and book clients will be a breeze.

Uranus in the Seventh House

Here Uranus inclines the person to do couples astrology or wedding electional astrology. Either way working with two people through their astrology will be a good fit if this is your Uranus house.

Uranus in the Eighth House

Exploring the deep psychological issues and traumas of life will be your forte with this Uranus house placement. You will be good a private sessions that bring your clients hidden angsts to light.

Uranus in the Ninth House

To teach others and lecture will be good for this placement of Uranus. Here there may be continual learning and exploration of astrology as a philosophy. You are likely to write and publish a book or books and papers on your astrological understanding.

Uranus in the Tenth House

This is the classic house placement to run an astrology business. You can achieve good success with astrology and become well known as an astrologer.

Uranus in the Eleventh House

This placement suggest that you will be good in group work perhaps in your local astrology gathering or by setting up Meetup and get-togethers for other astrologers. This placement suggests you can collaborate with small groups in your astrology business.

Uranus in the Twelfth House

This placement does support research astrology and private sessions. You may not wish to broadcast that you do astrology and keep a low profile.

Your Uranus Aspects

All aspects to Uranus will indicate the type of astrology that you can do and will be good at. These aspects can also show where you will be challenged and tested in your business. Any planet in aspect to Uranus suggests how you do (and can) use Uranus, and therefore astrology, in your life. Consider the aspect itself and only look at the Ptolemaic aspects of conjunction, sextile, square, trine and opposition. Ignore minor or lesser used aspects with the exception of the quintile.

Uranus Conjunctions

Planets conjoined Uranus can suggest the true nature of your astrology interest. Any planet in this position will influence your astrology and shows what excites you about astrology.

Uranus Sextiles

Any planet sextile Uranus shows your latent talents in astrology in the nature of the planet making the sixty degree aspect. Pay attention to any sextiles as they indicate where you will be good and gifted.

Uranus Squares

Squares to Uranus indicate that you have to overcome astrological issues in the nature of the planet. You may be challenged by the planet and its meaning in your astrological beliefs or have to work through what the planet means in your business. This can suggest your clients are tense.

Uranus Trines

Planets trine Uranus indicate that you will be very good at the things shown by the trining planet. Your astrological business can benefit if you embrace what the planet in trine suggests.

Uranus Oppositions

Planets which oppose your Uranus can point to obstacles that you have to overcome in order to get your astrology business going. These issues could be regulatory (that is in the registering of your business) or just show the type of person whom you will attract to your practice.

Uranus Quintiles

Planets in a quintile aspect to your Uranus show where you have astrological creativity and genius. This will be expressed by the planet making the quintile, its nature and condition. Any planet quintile Uranus is indicative of how you will shine in astrology and you would do well to make a careful assessment of this planet.

Your Uranus Direction

Uranus Direct

When Uranus is direct it is good for an astrology practice and the development of it as a part of your life. You can move forward at a regular and steady pace. You will gain and grow an astrology business on a steady trajectory throughout your life. Perhaps you will add to your abilities and take further courses yourself to develop a deeper astrology knowledge.

Uranus Stationary

When Uranus is stationary in the natal chart you need to check if it is about to go direct or retrograde. Uranus in this position offers a strong presence for astrology where you really spend time to fully know your craft before being able to move on which usually happens later in life.

Uranus Retrograde

If Uranus is retrograde in your natal chart it suggests a slower or longer lead-up time to get going in a professional astrological career. This placement of Uranus inclines you to review and ponder your basic knowledge base (planets, signs, houses and aspects) for longer, before you feel confident. It is almost as if you are hesitant to go professional. If this is the case it is best for you to take formal classes in astrology and gain astrological certification, which will provide you with the confidence to move up a level.

Getting Started

This section is about the nuts and bolts of setting up an astrology business. Many of the features of this chapter can be used for any business start-up and not just your astrology business. The main principles are the same. As we are considering your astrology business which is, by its very nature, a one person show we can use your own birth chart for clues on how to proceed to create a prosperous astrology business tailored for you. We cover websites, business cards social media and the trappings of a business in general.

We do not cover country specific legal company set-ups and work permits etc. Please refer to your personal accountant or lawyer for guidance on these matters.

You and Your Sun

Your whole chart shows who you are, your life potential and natal promise. You as yourself is shown by your Sun and its condition.

The Sun is You

Physically the Sun is your heart which pumps the blood that keeps you alive. An ultrasound scan of a fetus will show the heart beating as the first sign of life. Your Sun and its condition, by sign, house and aspect, will show who you are.

Sun Signs Strengths

Some Sun signs are better suited to the nature of the Sun.

- The strongest Sun sign is Leo where the Sun is in dignity.
- A dynamic Sun sign is Aries where the Sun is exalted and trine Leo.
- A robust Sun sign is Sagittarius being both fire and trine Leo and Aries.
- A medium strength Sun sign is Gemini which is both air and sextile Leo.
- The moderate Sun signs are Cancer, Virgo, Capricorn and Pisces, which are all passive and in the twelfth harmonic (the signs semi-sextile and quincunx Leo).
- The steady Sun signs are Taurus and Scorpio which are both passive and square Leo.
- A compromised Sun sign is Libra where the Sun is found in its fall.
- The weakest Sun sign is Aquarius where the Sun is in the sign of its detriment and opposite Leo.

Sun's House

The Sun is strong in any of the four angular houses which are the first, fourth, seventh and tenth houses.

Gauquelin Sectors

If the Sun is in the Gauquelin sectors of a chart, that is within ten degrees either side of the Ascendant or the Midheaven, it is well placed.

Singleton by Hemisphere

If the Sun is a singleton by hemisphere it is stronger.

Bucket or Fan Handle

If the Sun is placed as the handle of a bucket of a fan shaped chart it gains weight.

Chart Ruler

If Leo is the sign on the Ascendant, it makes the Sun the chart ruler and this is a powerful position for the Sun. It is unlikely that any other planet will be stronger than the Sun if it is the chart ruler.

Sun's Aspects

Sun **conjunctions** support you in the nature of the planet making the conjunction.

Sun **sextiles** show your latent talents in line with the planet in sextile to the Sun.

Sun **squares** show your internal challenges suggested by the planet forming the square.

Sun **trines** show your natural abilities as suggested by the planet making the trine aspect although you may take them for granted.

Sun **oppositions** indicate external challenges that you face in the nature of the planet.

Your Sun's Overall Strength and Character

Have a full understanding of who you are as shown by your Sun and by that your character.

Aspiring Astrologer Activity – Your Sun

Your Sun's house.

Your Sun's sign.

Your Sun's aspects.

List five words that describe your character as shown by your natal Sun.

Your Name as Given

Your Birth Name

Your name was chosen by your parents and given to you at birth. Therefore, it is related to your birth chart. You may keep the exact name conferred on you or shorten it like having Elizabeth but shortening it to Liz.

In astrology we use your common name which is the one you go by. So, if your name is Jessica Rabbit do you use Jess, Jesse, Jessie or Jessica in business? It is up to you.

Your Given Name

I believe it is best to use your given name for business purposes. So, in legal documents like company registrations and your business cards use your given name.

Women who take their husband's name in marriage can use either their maiden name or their married name. If you get divorced and married again you can use any of the surnames you have legally had.

I knew a woman call Olivia Jones she married a guy called Alex Twister. She kept her maiden name for business purposes because she did not want to be known as Olivia Twister.

Conferring Your Name

Remember in Harry Potter, Voldemort, he whose name cannot be said. They did not want to say his name because to do so was to invoke Voldemort's power.

Every time your name is spoken it adds power to you. When your name is said out loud it confers power to you. If others gossip about you it adds power to you. If you gossip about others you add power to them.

Be aware of who you talk about and be careful when you discuss your competition because you can make them stronger by repeating their names.

Pseudonyms and pen names

If you feel the need to hide behind your name set your new "astrology" name at the outset. Choose a business name and stick to it.

Aspiring Astrology Activity

Write down the name you will use in your astrology business.

Your Midheaven - Your Business

Find a Business Name that Means Something

It is best to find a business name that means something. Businesses are entities all to themselves and astrology sees them as such. Every time someone says your name it confers a blessing on you. The more the name is repeated the stronger it becomes. This is how names work.

The powerful essence in a name can be seen when parents choose a name for their children. Much thought goes into selecting a name in line with their family traditions, faith or culture. Parents do not pick a girl's name for a boy and vice versa. They choose a name that they want their child to grow up to be, to develop into or that which they aspire for their offspring. Make sure you labor under the umbrella of a well thought out business name. Plan for your future and get a great name.

Your Midheaven

Each sign and planetary ruler has a color, jewel, metal or mineral associated with it. The Midheaven sign and ruler are clues on how to name your business. This information varies depending on which astrology tradition you follow and use the outer planets or not. You may find other jewels, metal and minerals associated with the planets.

Planet: Color - Jewel - Metal and or Mineral

Sun: Yellow - peridot - gold.

Moon: White - pearl and mother-of-pearl - silver.

Mercury: Green - tiger's eye - quicksilver or platinum.

Venus: Pink - emerald - copper and coinage metals.

Mars: Red - ruby - iron and ferrous metals.

Jupiter: Royal blue - sapphire - tin and aluminum.

Saturn: Black and grey - jet and onyx - lead and fossils.

Uranus: Electric blue - amethyst - uranium and fool's gold.

Neptune: Cyan - crystal and opal - coral and sea shells.

Pluto: Maroon - garnet - titanium and oil.

Aspiring Astrologer Activity - Midheaven

Note your Midheaven sign.

State which planet is your Midheaven ruler.

List your Midheaven aspects.

How to Select Your Business Name

When you start out in business you need a name. The corporate experts recommend not naming any business from your own initials like PJ's Astrology or KY's Astrology.

To find a new name for your astrology business may take several days or even a few weeks. Begin with a list of options that appeal to you and work the words together to find a brief list of three possible business names.

Say the front runner names out loud and ask yourself:

- Do the names roll off your tongue?
- Can you say them on the phone?
- Does the person at the other end immediately know how to spell them?
- Are they hard to write?
- Are they similar to someone else's name? Let us not have Amazon Astrology either.
- Write the name backwards as this can expose unexpected results.

And the winner is…

Write your three finalists on a piece of paper.

Then sleep on it. Yes, that is right, tuck the paper under your pillow and go to sleep. The next morning pay attention to what immediately springs to your mind. Follow your instincts. It is your business.

Aspiring Astrologer Activity

Write your business name.

Your Tag Line

Your Tag Line

A tag line is one sentence that states what your business is about. A tag line is in simple terms and can be understood by anyone. Your tag line can be used on all promotional materials, your website and business cards. It is like a sub-heading to your business name. A tag line is sometimes called a strap line.

Aspiring Astrologer Activity – Tag Line

Write your business name from the previous section.

Write your tag line below it.

Your Domain Name

A domain name is the name of your internet site. Well-known examples are www.apple.com, www.bbc.com or www.richardbranson.com. When we talk about personal astrology sites you usually have something like www.yourname.com where yourname is the name of your astrology business.

As you begin to build your astrology practice the choice of your domain name is critical. You will live with this name for a long time so try to get it right at the outset. Changes in your domain name once established are not recommended.

What to Have in Your Domain Name

Have the word "astrology" in the name because this helps Google find you as an astrologer.

Make it something you can easily spell over the phone. (Think Cruise and Cruz).

Choose a name with meaning for you.

Include the theme of your business to indicate whether it is psychological, soul-purpose, esoteric, evolutionary or another type of astrology.

Sometimes you have to create a new word as we did with Starzology.

What Not to Have as Your Domain Name

Avoid using your initials as in PJ's Astrology and KY's Astrology. Think about it.

Do not choose a name similar to someone else's name like www.googleastrology.com or www.darksunastrology.com (there is a wonderful astrology site called www.darkstarastrology.com). If you do use a domain name similar to someone else's it adds confusion for your readers and the other guy will be miffed.

Domain Name Extensions

Watch out for taking www.fredsastrology.com if there is already a www.fredsastrology.ca. Other extensions are .com, .net and .org to look out for and there are several more domain name extensions with the list growing all the time.

If you can, get the .com extension as that is the norm and refers to a commercial (or business site) and it sets you up for a strong future presence.

Clarity and Purpose in Domain Names

Starzology is my main astrology site where I broadcast; how I see astrology, my thoughts on running an astrology business and a selection of aspects about astrology.

For example, my niche topics include:

- Living an authentic life in-line with your natal chart
- Your astrology business
- The oriental planet
- Dispositor trees
- Children's astrology
- Vocational astrology
- Finding the creativity in your chart.

Starzology is a niche astrology site and not really a mainstream astrology site because the focus is not on "horoscopes" for the general public.

Years ago, my team and I brainstormed the domain name Starzology which we created when we lived in Oakville near Toronto. I was able to port (transfer) it seamlessly to Vancouver when our family moved across the country.

Domain Name Ideas

- Try to have the extension .com.
- Try to have the word astrology in your domain name.
- Make it easy to say on the phone and spell - think Kozmik and Cosmic.
- Do not be similar to others so no Goggle.com or Gaggle.com.
- Do not use your initials.
- If necessary, invent a new word like Starzology.com.

Aspiring Astrologer Activity – Domain Name

Write your domain name and extension.

Your Website

If you are going into business as an astrologer, you need a website. Gone are the days when you could get away without one. If you do not know where to start take a class, get some lessons or get someone to set it up for you.

Self-hosting is Best

I recommend self-hosting, so you can name your domain correctly. I recommend Dreamhost.com for web hosting and you can ask them to load WordPress for you to use.

Pages and Posts

A page contains information that mainly stays the same as your biography and contact info. A post is actually a blog post, and this is where you can write all your feature articles and comments about the new moon or Jupiter changing signs or whatever is your astrological interest of the moment.

You will write your upcoming class details on your class page but the detail of each special class or event on a post.

Use pages to list classes you teach but posts to carry the class details.

Pages You Need on Your Website

You will need the following pages on your site.

- Home page
- About page
- Contact page
- Products page
- Services page
- Testimonials page
- Email list sign-up page
- Events page

Posts You Need on Your Website

Posts come in two forms, transit posts and evergreen posts.

Transit Post

A transit post is typically about astrology events that pass by like the new moon or Jupiter changing sign or the latest outer planet aspects and anything that happens in the astrology of the day that is coming up soon *and will pass.*

Eclipses are good examples of a transit post. Horoscopes for the day month or year are transit posts. They will only happen once and then pass. So, an eclipse piece you write this year will not be read next year.

Evergreen Post

An evergreen post is one that can be read again and again and is always relevant. Examples of evergreen posts are topics like signs, planets, houses and aspects.

You can write about special topics and here is where your niche topic or specialty comes into its own. I like the oriental planet and have written many posts about this topic. They are evergreen because they are as relevant today as the day when I wrote them.

Ideally you should have a mixture of transit posts and evergreen posts on your website. The best ratio is transits to evergreens 1:2, this means for every transit post you write you will compose two evergreen posts.

In this way your website will grow into a wealth of evergreen information over the years whereas if you only write transit posts (or horoscopes), when the time has gone the material is of no further use and will not be read again. No one wants to read the horoscope for Virgo for September 2005 anymore.

Important Parts to Create on Your Website

On day one of your website there are many activities to do. Some things need to be created immediately and other activities can wait for later.

Below is a list of the pages and posts that you can create when you start your website. These ideas can also be used for already formed website where you want to get your business on track.

I have also suggested some related activities that you can start. Building a website can become a passion and may become seductive. Take your time and you will get there in the end.

On Day One of the Life of Your Website

Create a Home Page

State exactly what your site is about what you do and what makes you different to other astrology sites. On this page you can have suitable keywords that search engines can use to find you.

Create an About Page

On your about page say what you can do for your clients, how you can help them. State why they should read your blog and why they should visit your site again.

Create a Contact Page

List your email address and general location. Do not give exact addresses. Make it easy for prospective clients to find you.

Create a Welcome Post

Your first post will welcome readers to your site. Here you can include what is coming up and what you will be focusing on in the next few weeks. You can write a teaser and give a glimpse of the good things to come.

Create an Astrology Topic Post

This will either be a transit post or an evergreen post. It needs to be on a topic that interests you in astrology, so you can write confidently and with passion. Share your love of astrology and put your heart into the words.

Load the Jetpack plugin

This is on WordPress and counts your visitors. Or get your webmaster to load some form of visitor monitoring.

Open a PayPal Account

You need to be able to process payments over the internet. PayPal is the most widely used payment processor that accepts credit cards but there are others like Stripe.

Find one that works for you and set it up, so you can receive payments.

In Week One of the Life of Your Website

Create a Consultations Page

Your consultations page shows the type of readings that you offer. Perhaps you do natal chart and forecasting. Here you can tell your clients exactly the type of astrology reading you offer.

State when and on which days you work and how long in hours each sessions or reading will be.

Create a Products Page

On your products page you can list any products you have for sale. Products are items such as calendars, artwork, candles or jewelry etc.

Your products are ready to sell now. On your products page you can highlight what will be available soon.

Create a Services Page

The services page lists other astrological services you could offer like rectification or wedding elections.

Create an Opinion Post

Write an opinion post on some feature of astrology on which you have a strong opinion. For example, you could write that you use the Porphry and not the Regiomantanus house system for mundane charts and explain why you do this.

Setup a MailChimp Account

This will be used for your mailing list, so you can keep in touch with your clients, students and fans.

In Month One of the Life of Your Website

Create a Testimonials Page

This page lists testimonials from satisfied clients and students or those for whom you have done astrology work in the past. Always ask for permission before printing a testimonial from someone.

Create an Email List Sign-up Page

This page is where readers go to sign up for your emails and newsletter. This is where MailChimp comes in.

To have a separate page allows strangers who have found you on the web to keep up with what you are doing. They may become clients in the future.

Create an Events Page

On your events page list all the places where you will speak, lecture or be in person.

For example. at radio and TV stations, where you will give a class or any workshop or conference you may be a speaker or even just attend.

Your events page shows where the public can interact with you.

Create a Forecast Post

Write a forecast post. This could perhaps be about the next solar eclipse and how it will affect people in each sign or something about an upcoming ingress or Mercury retrograde period or perhaps the next transiting yod that will form and what it means.

Do These Other Activities

Source More Images

You will continuously need images for your website. Every page and post must have at least one image. These images can be astrology charts if it is a transit post. If it is an evergreen post, you will need images as well.

You will require time to find pictures and diagrams for the pages and posts that you will publish so it is a good idea to have some up you sleeve for later.

Create a Content Calendar

A content calendar is a calendar which shows when you will publish your new posts. It is for your planning and is not public knowledge.

When you begin, plan to publish a post once a week on the day of the week that relates to the planetary ruler of your Midheaven.

If you Midheaven is Leo, publish on the Sun's day which is Sunday. If your Midheaven is Cancer, then publish on the Moon's day which is Monday.

Perhaps you decide to write about the Venus Mars synodic cycle. You could have a series of posts relating to this topic.

Example Content Calendar

Week 1 - Venus in general as an evergreen post.

Week 2 - Mars in general as an evergreen post.

Week 3 - The Venus Mars conjunction in general as an evergreen post.

Week 4 - The current Venus Mars conjunction at 27 Taurus as a transit post.

Linking Posts

Always add links in every post.

- Link the week 1 post to week 2, 3 and 4.
- Link the week 2 post to week 1, 3 and 4.
- Link the week 3 post to week 1, 2 and 4.
- Link the week 4 post to week 1, 2 and 3.

When your write other posts in the future that mention Venus you may link them to the Venus in general post (week 1).

When you write about Mars in the future you could consider linking back to the Mars in general post (week 2).

If you write about conjunctions in the future, you could link back to the Venus conjunct Mars post (week 3). In this way you build a network of links within in your website and it becomes easier for visitors to discover your content.

It is unlikely that you will ever link to the transit post about the Venus Mars conjunction at 27 Taurus ever again.

Your Email Addresses

When you set up a business there are a few email addresses that you will need. You can get by with one email address for a long time but think ahead and consider creating the others. When you set up your domain name you will need a few email addresses.

Your main everyday email address will be: firstname@yourdomainname.com

Your PayPal email address will be: payments@yourdomainname.com

Your general query email address will be: info@yourdomainname.com

Your assistant's email address will be: assistant@yourdomainname.com

Your webmaster's email address will be: webmaster@yourdomainname.com

Your Email Address

You can begin with yourname@yourdomainname.com

PayPal Email Address

To have a separate email address for your PayPal makes sense. PayPal will link one email address to one bank account at a time. If you have several mini-businesses which all astrology are related, then to have a central PayPal email address makes sense.

Webmaster Email Address

It is advised that you set up a separate webmaster email address for your domain as this is the industry standard for two reasons. You may engage an independent webmaster to design your site and they will require their own email address. Secondly, if there are errors with screens on the site your users will email the webmaster.

Aspiring Astrologer Activity

Write your main email address.

List any future email addresses you may use.

Your Email Signature

Make it easy for people to contact you. Do not make potential prospects have to dig about to find information about contacting you. The space at the end of an email is prime real estate for promotion and name recognition. You should not ignore the potential to engage your readership and clients further. You can do more with an email signature.

Your email signature is the two or three lines that go below your name at the end of each email. Every email you send has the potential to be forwarded to other people and this is where it is useful to place more information as the future receiver may not have heard of you, have internet access, or any other problem reading a forwarded email.

On Your Email Signature Add:

Your web address.

Your company name.

Your tag line.

Your phone number (optional).

Your city or area.

Your contact email.

Example email signature with detail:

Alison Price

Professional Astrologer

Starzology - Astrology with heart

Vancouver (downtown)

alison@starzology.com

Additional Topical Links in Your Email Signature

If you have a new exciting post, an astrology class starting, other event or special offer that will happen soon you can add those details in a one line link into your email signature.

For instance, you can add the line:

>Seasonal discount on readings until December 25th.

Make the line link to the page on your site with the special offer.

The details are on the webpage not the email signature. Your special offer will change over time and sometimes will not be relevant. If you have an event coming up always promote it in your email signature.

Aspiring Astrologer Activity

Write your email signature below.

Your Design

Your Design Elements

You will need some design for your website and other promotional items. Spend no more than one lunar cycle choosing your design elements then stick to them.

Colors

Choose two colors, one main and one secondary. Look to your Midheaven for ideas.

Fonts

Choose two fonts for your business. One serif (with curly tips) like Garamond and one sanserif (with no curly tips) like Helvetica Neue.

Your Mercury Element and Fonts

When you use words, you can do so after your Mercury by sign and placement. Mercury suggests the fonts you will choose in your branding and whether you will have lowercase letters, or script and serif fonts or bold and sans serif fonts.

- Mercury in fire signs likes flashy and creative fonts.
- Mercury in earth signs likes heavy and bold fonts.
- Mercury in air signs likes cool and light fonts.
- Mercury in water signs likes soft and gentle fonts.

Logos

A logo is a small (usually square) image that can be used to give the impression of your business without saying a word. Your logo can be used on all social media and business cards and even embroidered onto caps, bags and other merchandise.

Artwork

You can get artwork in your design and color palette which can be used in larger promotional places.

For example, in the banner at the top of your webpage, and as big banners hanging in an astrology booth at a New Age fair.

Your Business Card

Business Cards

A business card is a must if you have a business. If you do not have a business card you are seen as an amateur.

Choose a white or ivory card and black print, or, use your designs two colors and fonts.

What to Print on your Business Card:

- First name, middle initial and last name.
- Type of astrologer (optional).
- Phone number including area code.
- Email address.
- Suburb, city, state/province and country (No exact address).
- Print your logo on your card.

Your Brand

Your Brand is Who you Are and What you Do

Your brand is shown in your style, presence, colors and interests. You see your brand in the type of work you do and services you are selling.

Your Brand

For example, you may be an astrologer, but you could specialize in party astrology, or you may be a horoscope writer with virtually no clients in the broad sense.

How to Define your Brand

You are different to the next astrologer. You provide a unique service. Maybe you teach or write books. Maybe you only work with women's charts or sports astrology. Perhaps your clients are businessmen seeking market tips. You have to know who you are.

Consider doctors. All doctors can be general practitioners or family GP's, but some are dermatologists and others are brain surgeons, some focus on diet and others on fitness. But, all are doctors in the end. They could all probably save your life if they walked past you in a car accident.

We know which type of doctor each one is by their brand and their branding.

To find your brand you have to do the same for your astrology practice. Decide who you are, and who you are not, astrologically.

Your Chart

Your natal chart suggests who you are seen as being in general (Midheaven), who you are seen as one-on-one (ascendant) and who you could be seen as (oriental planet).

Your Platform

What is Your Platform?

Your platform is your reach. It is the amount of people you know, today, either; in person, by being clients, or those who want your emails, or to whom you are linked on social media. Your reach is the number of people to whom you can write an astrology email today and which they will open and read.

Aspiring Astrologer Activity

Calculate your reach now:

- Number of clients (all time) =
- Number of people on your mailing list =
- Number of "friends" on social media =
- Number of people in your live audiences =
- Other =

Add them all together to get your total reach =

You grow your platform one person at a time. Everything you do from today onwards is aimed a growing your platform. Check the number of your reach at every cardinal ingress to see how you have improved.

Grow Your Platform and Grow your Business

Great platforms reach more than 20000 people.
Good platforms reach more than 2000 people.
Flimsy platforms reach more than 200 people.
Weak platforms reach less than 200 people.

How to Build Your Platform

"Build your platform one plank at a time. Then stand on it."

"The bigger your platform the further your reach."

Platform

In days gone an old-fashioned soapbox was where a guy stood and shouted his message at the milling crowd. Maybe he is yelling the headlines and then catches the passerby's attention and sells them a newspaper. See how it works. The passer-by walks the same route every day. He will even cross over the road to pick up the paper. If the guy's message is compelling enough, and it piques the pedestrian's interest. These days your passing crowd are those who hear your message. Your passersby are the basis for your platform and they are measured in several ways.

Your Reach

Your platform is the number of people to whom you reach out, or can touch, on a daily basis through social media, networking and direct contact as face-to-face and via email.

- Your reach is who you can influence.
- Your reach includes those who "get" your message.
- Your reach is those who believe in what you have to say.
- Your reach is those who want to speak your language.

Your platform does not include your Mom.

Know your People - your Tribe

Who are your keepers, clients and readers? Who are your followers? Your followers may not be whom you think. Find out about those who do interact with you. Tweak your message to tune into your followers.

Your Ideal Client

Know the qualities you want in your ideal client.

Consider such factors as their age group, gender, interests, marital status, economic group, children and other features of your ideal client that interests you.

Get a picture of your ideal client and keep them in mind as you work.

Aspiring Astrologer Activity - Platform

What type of platform do you have today?

What type of platform do you want in 12 months' time?

List features of your idea client.

Your Biography

You need to create two biographies for your astrology business, a short one and a long one.

Short Biography of 100 Words

Have a short biography of about 100 words ready. Your short bio will include your main website URL's and publications. Make every word count without any fluff or waffle and keep it simple, short and sweet.

Your short bio is used at the end of published print articles and on your gravatar for your website posts and any guest posts you write.

Long Biography of 250 Words

Create a long biography of about 250 words. This has more detail and highlights your top astrological accomplishments and your astrological philosophy.

You can mention the type of astrology you practice and say what you can do for others and your clients. Include your main website URL's and contact email details.

Your long bio should be placed on your about page below the main content.

Your more detailed biography can be read by prospective clients who want to get to know you a little better before contacting you for a reading. You can be warm and genuine here.

What to Include in Your Biographies

Always include and relevant qualifications, and only your astrological qualifications, or something in a related field like Tarot or psychology. Be positive and upbeat.

Married - check

Loves dogs – check

Be human, but do not do an exposé on your life. Be cool.

What Not to Include in Your Biographies

Do not include any irrelevant qualifications. If you are a qualified scuba diver, we do not need to know it in your astrology bio. Ignore your life-saving certificate, degree in civil engineering or your karate black belt info.

If you drink beer every Friday night, do not include this in your bio. That you are the local hot dog eating champion is also not suitable content for your astrological bio.

Your Journey - Optional

A "Your journey" piece is all about how you arrived at astrology and how it has changed your life.

I believe that a deep exploration and the motives that created your life-direction is not really suitable information for the two biographies listed above.

Your journey story has a place.

Your journey piece can turn into a blog post. This will ultimately become a part of your brand and image in the public eye.

Aspiring Astrologer Activity – Bio

Write a short and a long bio for yourself.

Your Promotional Photo

A promotional photo, or promo photo, is typically a headshot, or a head and shoulders photograph of you and you alone.

You will need a good color photograph and not just one taken from your phone or laptop camera.

You can set aside a morning and be nicely dressed and made up and have someone help you. Take your time, take many shots and get a really good photo. You will use it for years to come.

The best images are taken in morning light before noon.

Where to Use Your Promo Photo

On your business card.

On your local astrology groups "about you" page.

On your written books back cover.

On the lecture handouts you distribute at conferences and workshops.

In articles you write.

On your website.

When you guest post on other websites.

On all promotional information and flyers.

On all merchandise goods, tarot cards, magnets or pens etc.

On huge banners at fairs.

What to Have in Your Promo Photo

- You.
- You with a smile.
- Good lighting.
- Neat hair.
- Neutral clothes that do not overpower your face.
- Subdued jewelry, especially earrings.

What Not to Have in Your Promo Photo

- Do not have other people in the shot like your partner or your kids.
- Your dog or cat.
- No fussy backgrounds or jazzy wallpaper.
- Sunglasses.
- Hats.
- You, eating food.

Your Photo Library

A photo library is a page on your website with photos of you at work and at business related events. In your photo library there will be images of you speaking, writing, at your desk or perhaps at a book signing. You may even snap shots when travelling to conferences simply at the airport or going about your day.

You need photos for your own website. Remember all images that you load to your own website must be taken by you, be owned by you or free or commons.

You may wish to go to a free image site or buy pictures from a paid image site. Do not scrape the web and lift other people's images.

Other people will search for images of you if you are presenting or doing something in public for them and these need to be in your photo library.

Photos you Need in Your Photo Library

- Your promo headshot in color.
- Your promo headshot in black and white.
- You working at your desk.
- You at astrology events like classes, lectures and parties etc.
- Charts you have worked on or other data sheets such as bi-wheels etc.
- Any products you sell like calendars, astrological art, coffee mugs and jewelry etc.

Always take photos of yourself when you are at an astrology related event because you never know when and where you can use them later.

Your One Page Information Sheet

Each astrologer is different to the next astrologer and we are not all the same nor do we offer identical skills, products or readings. You can create your "One Page" info sheet to show where the focus of your astrology contribution lies.

On your One Page Info Sheet you can gather all the information others may need about what you offer in terms of courses, consultations and services. It should include most of the things you do although there may be more on your website.

Who Reads Your One Page Info Sheet

This is for those prospective clients who would like to get to know you a bit better and wondered what else you have to offer.

It is also for those who want to invite you to speak at their next event, meeting, workshop or conference.

Your Elevator Pitch

An elevator pitch is a way that businesses can quickly provide information about their products and services all in the time it takes to ride an elevator. This is about sixty seconds.

For those of you not in North America it would probably be called a lift pitch but that somehow does not have the same ring to it.

Not everyone understands the difference between newspaper Sun Sign column astrology and the deep interpretive astrology you provide. You have to explain your philosophy, outlook, orientation and that you love what you do.

Most prospective clients want to partner with engaged people so make sure you set the right tone in your message. You are not writing dry legal copy (yawn) so use vibrant, dare I say juicy, words that appeal to others on an emotional level.

Say everything you need to say in the time limit of under one minute. An elevator pitch usually works out to between 75 to 150 words and on average is 100 words.

Components of Your Astrological Elevator Pitch

State all the important information about the benefits to your client of your astrology business. The words have to be understandable by anyone (especially non-astrologers) when you meet them for the first time.

You have to say it all during the time it takes to ride an elevator. Once you have the words on the page you can practice saying them in front of a mirror.

Clarity is Everything at This Stage

Condensing what may be a complicated process (doing astrological charts and readings) into a clear message which is understandable to a regular person is the aim. Do not use astrologese. Keep it simple.

Your Natal Jupiter

The planet of promotion is Jupiter. Look at your natal Jupiter's condition by sign, dispositor, house and tight Ptolemaic aspects to search for ideas on how to promote yourself in this way.

Where to Use your Elevator Pitch

It is like what we used to say of having a good patter which means getting your business message across quickly and clearly. Your carefully crafted elevator pitch can be used immediately in the following areas in your business

Use Your Elevator Pitch when Speaking

When you meet people.

When you meet other astrologers.

At a cocktail party.

When pitching yourself on the phone.

When introducing yourself at a presentation.

Use Your Elevator Pitch in Print:

In your gravatar biographical info.

In your promotional brochures.

In any "about me" spot on social media.

In any workshop flyers.

On your website bio page.

In the foreword of your book.

As part of your email signature.

My Example Elevator Pitch

"I am a professional astrologer who mentors a selection of engaged astrology students each year. I have fun helping you create a successful astrology business and to show you how to solve the two main issues facing astrologers which are how to move from student to professional astrologer status and how to develop, establish and manage a small business. I love doing children's work and to help you with your career or business coaching. It all comes from my heart and with a sense of humor. I invite you to contact me at alison@starzology.com."

This elevator pitch is only 90 words but can be expanded to suit the situation. Note that it is the essence of what I do. No more, no less.

Aspiring Astrologer Activity – Elevator Pitch

Write a 100 word elevator pitch for yourself.

Your Social Media Presence

Social media is all the online places you hang out like Facebook, Twitter, LinkedIn, Instagram, Pinterest or YouTube. There are many others as well. By its very nature the list of social media opportunities changes all the time as one platform grows in popularity and another diminishes.

If you are not yet on social media, you need to get going for your business social media.

Every social media post should have a link back to your site. Your website is like the mothership. Everything you do off your website must always feed back to the mothership.

Start Your Business Social Media

You need a business Facebook page. This is not your regular social page where you are friends with your Mom, sisters and old boyfriends. You need a special business Facebook page which is separate and where you post about only astrology.

- Get a Twitter business handle for all your business related tweets.
- Begin a business Pinterest board.
- Start a business Instagram presence.
- Open a business YouTube channel.

What to Post on Business Social Media

Do post about:

- Your specialty in astrology.
- Any new and exciting blog posts you make.
- Details about any classes you are giving.
- Transit or New Moons etc.
- Where you will be speaking, in person, on the radio or TV.
- Seasonal discounts like Christmas and back-to-school specials etc.

What Not to Post on Business Social Media

- Do not comment about what you had for lunch or your trip to the dermatologist.
- Do not post independently on social media without having the main body of the text on your site with a link to it.

Your Solar Fire Compliments Text

The astrology program Solar Fire has a spot for your compliments and I expect that the other astrology programs offer the same feature. This vital information can be printed on all your charts.

In Solar Fire go to [settings], [compliments] to change and edit the default compliments text to your choice of words. You have five lines for your compliments, so it is important to make each line count. The first line will be bold.

Print your Solar Fire compliments text on every chart you print or send digitally to clients.

Suggestions:

Astrology by (Your name).

Type of astrologer.

Business name / website name / tag line.

Email address.

Phone number (optional).

Example Solar Fire Compliments Text

Professional astrology by Alison Price

Starzology – Astrology with heart

alison@starzology.com

Keep it Fresh

Always keep your compliments text up to date. Edit and refresh your message once a year as you do your annual business review. You can tweak it during the year if anything changes.

Astrology Software Compliments Text in General

I expect other astrology programs have this possibility as well. The point is that you need to promote your business where you can.

A printed chart will lie in a file or at your client's home for years. Your contact details will still be there. Make sure they are reflective of who you are and your business.

How to Find Clients

It may seem the most difficult thing in the world to find clients. How and who become your clients have much to do with the internal dynamics of your own chart.

In a world of millions of people to find your customers, people and those whom you can reach may seem daunting.

This chapter looks at how to find clients and not just any clients but those who want to be helped by you and those who love your message.

Own Your Niche

Your Niche is Your Specialty

You cannot be everything to everyone. Choose a particular branch of astrology or a specific group of clients that interest you and cultivate them.

How to Find Your Astrological Niche

Uranus is the modern ruler of astrology and your natal Uranus and its complex (placement by sign, house and aspects) will show you the type of astrology you are likely to find interesting or that you naturally are good at and will gravitate towards.

Aspiring Astrologer Activity

Circle everything that interests you about astrology and add more.

Consulting

Psychological

Podcasts

Asteroids

Natal Charts

Eclipses

Retrogrades

Stations

Teaching astrology

Planets

Horoscopes

Research

Sun Sign column

Houses

History Mundane

Financial astrology

Signs

Astronomy for astrologers

Video horoscopes

Aspects

Bereavement astrology

Audio horoscopes

Transits

Evolutionary astrology

Chinese astrology

Magazine astrology

Uranian astrology

Jayne's hypotheticals

Couples astrology

TV astrology

Radio astrology

Hellenistic

Local space time

Career astrology

Progressions

Conference owner

Vedic astrology

Teaching astrology

Trans Neptunian objects

Local group volunteer

Women's astrology

Moiety

National group work

Solar returns

Harmonics

Decumbiture

Declinations

Lunar nodes

Planetary nodes

North American astrology

Western astrology

Own Your Niche

When you find your niche become the best expert in that niche. Become a specialist in one area and know everything there is to know about that particular niche.

Your Products and Services

Products

All items and goodies that you create, make and sell are your products. Products can be sold when you are not there and can be sold by others. Products are ready to sell now.

Your Products may Include:

- Your written horoscope column as a digital download.
- MP3's, audios, videos, taped webinars or podcasts of talks.
- eBooks and physical books.
- Astrology artwork, knick-knacks, calendars, candles and cards etc.

Services

Your services are things you offer but are those which you have to attend to yourself. Services can only happen (be sold) if you are there in person.

Your services may be any of the following:

- An in-person client consultation (natal and forecast etc.)
- A written report for a client (written by you).
- A lecture, a talk or workshop (presented by you).
- Rectification or electional services.
- The teaching of a class or lesson.
- Webinars in person.
- Meet and greets.

Aspiring Astrologer Activity: Your products and Services

List all the products you presently have.

List all the products you would like to have.

List the services you presently have,

List all the services you would like to have.

How Your Natal Chart Attracts Clients

Where do Clients come From?

Astrology students who think of starting their practice often ask me "Where do clients come from?"

This really is a query any independent business owner will pose. It is the whole point of doing what you do and to sell your products and services, but to whom and where are these people?

Where do you find your first client or indeed your second and third?

Maybe you Need some Advertising

There are several traditional ways to advertise and attract astrology clients such as:

- An advert in your local newspaper.
- A promotional piece in new age trade magazines.
- As a flyer in an esoteric bookshops.
- Mentioning your services at your local astrology group.
- Word of mouth.

By far and away the best form of advertising for an astrologer is word of mouth. This is so for three reasons:

Personal reference is best, personal reference is best and personal reference is best.

Why Personal Reference is Best

- The person who refers you is a past client and has been to see you already. They have the inside track on exactly what goes on at a reading.
- They refer you because they like you, what you have to say and your style.
- They want their friend or family member to like you and your reading as well.
- Clients who come to you via a personal reference are pre-sold on astrology.

The take home from this is that you have to look after your first client. They are the portal to new business. They can easily become repeat business. This is critical. You need to treat every client as you do your first client to grow your business.

Your Chart Attracts Your Clients

If we accept that you are your chart and the placements and connections in your nativity show who you are and the potentials you have to become in this lifetime, then it follows that you will attract the clients you need by the nature of your chart.

Say, you enter a room with ten people lined up. Immediately you are attracted to one or two, you are not attracted to one or two and the remaining six people well, they could go either way. This instinctive attract or repel comes from your chart. You are attracted to the other person's natal chart energies and how they integrate or fit in with yours.

They say, "You choose your friends and not your relatives" and the friends you do select suit you and your chart. Like a jigsaw puzzle, you add a piece each time you make a friend. They have to fit with you and with your chart. Your clients want to fit with you and indeed they are happy when they do.

You are Your Chart

As you go through life you project your ascendant outwards followed by the rest of your chart in varying degrees. Naturally others respond to it. This is known as synastry.

There is no point in looking towards other astrologers and trying to emulate their business success (at least not in a detailed way) as their birth chart is intrinsically different yours.

There are many books on business and that is a subject in itself. Here I am trying to show you how to use your very own talents as shown by your unique birth chart which is the astrologer's edge. I urge you to try it.

How to Find Clients

Your Clients

Your Moon (the public) and your seventh house (other people) show your clients. Simple, or not. Your chart is different to my chart and we both attract a distinct set of clients. The synastry between you and your clients is shown by the cross chart contacts and especially conjunctions.

As an astrologer, when your Sun is placed in your client's natal houses you will influence them as follows:

First house - You may influence them as a life coach.

Second house - You may help them with financial and self-worth issues.

Third house - You may educate clients about themselves as their teacher.

Fourth house - You may help them see their family dynamics.

Fifth house - You may be fun for them.

Sixth house - You may influence their work, health and daily rituals.

Seventh house - You may appreciate their marital issues and be a business partner.

Eighth house - You may change them on a fundamental, deep and personal level.

Ninth house - You may guide their education and growth as their guru.

Tenth house - You may offer career and life direction advice.

Eleventh house - You may be seen as a friend, associate and confidante.

Twelfth house - You may be privy to their very private and personal secrets.

Your Outer Planet Signature

Outer Planet Customers

The outer planets are Uranus, Neptune and Pluto. They can work on a subconscious level and determine who you attract. It is useful to know which of the outer planets is prominent for consciously seeking out the very customers we are naturally attracting.

It is a matter of engaging your Mercury to work your dominant outer planet by bringing it into your day-to-day thoughts. The outer planet energies are expressed in their own specific way.

What your Outer Planet Signature says about Your Clients

Not all business methods work for all businesses. Not all astrology business' work the same for everyone either. What gels with for one practitioner will not necessarily pan out for another because the two astrologers have different natal charts to each other.

To find satisfying work, you have to be aligned with the energy potentials shown in your own chart. One way of tapping into this is by looking at your outer planet signature.

Mercury

The idea is to engage your Mercury and get your conscious brain to work to bring the potentials of your prominent outer planet to bear on attracting the type of clients you want, and need, as shown by your natal chart.

We cannot all offer the same thing, but if you work with the astrology in your chart rather than against it you will be more satisfied in your craft.

Determine Which Outer Planet is Dominant

Chart signatures are usually assessed by looking at all the planets in the chart. This time we will only look at the outer planets to get an insights into how you work on a more subconscious level.

You want to find out what happens when you are not looking and paying attention. Your prominent outer planet will function almost as the background noise or default mode of your personal attraction.

You can discover which outer planet is strong in your natal chart by measuring which of them is more energized and engaged in your natal chart by checking with the following questions.

Aspiring Astrologer Activity

Answer the following questions for all three outer planets (Uranus, Neptune and Pluto) and add up your score at the end.

- It is your chart ruler? (15 points)
- Is it conjunct your ascendant? (15 points)
- Is it conjunct your Sun? (10 points)
- Is it conjunct your Moon? (10 points)
- Is it conjunct your chart ruler? (10 points)
- Is it conjunct your Midheaven? (10 points)
- Is it in accidental dignity? (5 points)
- Is it in your first house? (5 points)
- Is it direct? (5 points)
- Is it your oriental planet? (5 points)
- Is it the focal planet in a T-square? (5 points)
- Is it your most elevated planet? (5 points)

Usually the planet Uranus, Neptune or Pluto will step forward when you do a quick arithmetic calculation for each planet.

Your Outer Planet Signature

If you did the activity on the previous page you will have a number which represents the prominence of the outer planet in your chart.

So, what?

Well now you can see the difference in how each of the outer planets operate. Your strong outer planet will work for you over and above the two weaker outer planets in the following manner.

If the outer planet is not strong in the natal chart because say, the Moon dominates the chart, then the outer planetary energy will continue to operate the background of your life.

A Pluto Signature: Your Clients Magnetically Appear

If you have a strong Pluto, you can attract clients who:

- Find you by your cryptic messages in adverts.
- Magnetically appear.
- May hover in the shadows.
- May be afraid to approach you.
- May be lurkers before becoming clients.
- Come out of the woodwork and find you.

How to Promote Your Astrology Business with a Strong Pluto:

- Offer in-depth psychological readings.
- Offer sexual problem explorations.
- Promote the mystery of your craft.
- Offer private readings.
- Allow your clients anonymity.
- Stress your privacy policy.
- Offer deep insights.
- Explore past-life regressions.
- Offer bereavement astrology.

A Neptune Signature: Your Clients Intuitively Appear

If you have a strong Neptune outer planet energy you can attract clients who:

- Appreciate your arty adverts.
- Pray for help.
- Arrive by osmosis.
- Find astrology hypnotic.
- Believe in astrology.
- Are spiritually minded.

How to Promote Your Astrology Business with a Strong Neptune:

- Say you understand.
- Use your intuition.
- Offer a sympathetic ear.
- Say that you relate to them.
- Mention your belief in their problems.
- Intimate that you are a psychic or a medium (if you are).
- Use a crystal ball as a prop.
- Say you can help clients find their vision.

A Uranus Signature: Clients Suddenly Appear

If you have a strong Uranus outer planet signature in your birth chart you can attract clients who:

- Like astrology itself.
- Want to learn astrology.
- Are modern and up-to-date.
- Contact you at a group meeting.
- Use social networking.
- Like to be unusual.
- Think they can change the world.
- Are young up and coming professionals.

How to promote your astrology business if you have a strong Uranus outer planet signature:

- Promote astrology for the twenty-first century.
- Be New Age.
- Use a computer and techie props.
- Stress astrology is for young people.
- Promote astrology for the masses.
- Read futures.
- Break down borders.
- Support Astrologers without borders.
- Promote your astrology group.

These techniques can help you find the clients you can and want to help and work with.

How to Take A Booking

Your First Client Booking

When you start an astrology business you will have clients or customers who need to meet with you face-to-face for their reading or consultations. Up until now your friends have said, "Oh, please read my chart, what do you see?"

One difference between an amateur and a professional astrologer is that you have to have a system set up to take a booking.

There are a few things you need to know before taking a booking:

- Know your availability.
- Know how long the reading will be.
- Know what you can do and what you cannot do.
- Know your prices.

First Contact

Clients will speak to you face-to-face, through a mutual friend as a personal contact or email you as strangers. You need contact them or email them back within the next day or two and let them know when you can see them and offer them some timing options.

What You Need from Your Client

For all astrology work you will need from your client:

- Their full name.
- Their birth date as the day, month and year.
- Their birth time in hours and minutes and whether morning or afternoon.
- Their birthplace as in the town and country.
- The place they are living in now the town and country.

- Their email address.
- Phone number and or optional physical address.

You may want to send them a client registration form to complete and sign beforehand.

The Consultation Time and Date

A client consultation is usually booked for one hour, but it may overrun a bit. Give yourself enough time between accepting the booking and when you do the reading, so you can:

- Cast and print the charts.
- Interpret the chart.

Ask If There a Special Focus

You need to know if there is a focus for their appointment. If there is a specific question they want you to analyze or other areas in their life which needs an in-depth interpretation (often money, romance and health come up), ask your client to tell you as soon as possible so you can be fully prepared.

Most people have a specific reason to approach an astrologer.

Tell your client what to bring

If you do not record the sessions then tell your client that if they wish to record the session they may bring a digital recorder, phone or other device. I personally do not tape but my clients are most welcome to do so.

You client may want to take notes as well, so perhaps they could arrive with their writing materials. If it is an extended session or, they have travelled hundreds of miles to see you, your client may wish to bring a snack or their lunch.

Tell Your Client What Not to Bring

Let your client know that it will be a private consultation and that they should not bring a "friend" to sit in on the consultation. I also ask them not to bring their dog as one client of mine did. The fact that I had my own dog (who was not impressed with the visiting dog) did not help.

You May Offer Refreshments

A consultation is really about chatting for over an hour so in this time you can both get parched. You may wish to be prepared and provide a drink or at least water.

I usually offer regular tea or coffee and cookies, and I tell my clients so that if they wish they may bring their own specialty tea bags. I have the tray ready and the kettle boiled before they walk in, so it is quick to pour and sit down. I also have chilled iced water for my clients on a tray in the room before they arrive.

Tell Them About Your Privacy Policy

All consultations are strictly confidential. Even if your clients and you have mutual friends let them know beforehand that you respect their privacy and that you will not discuss their chart with anyone.

Tell Your Clients How to Pay

You may wish to get the payment after the reading or take a deposit. I always ask for the payment at the booking time. I will send them a PayPal invoice beforehand to their PayPal email address which is often different to their main email address.

Always Email to Acknowledge and Confirm the Booking

Send an acknowledgement email which states the time, date and venue of the consultation. You may also wish to confirm their birth data especially if they set the consultation up with you verbally and you had to write their birth date down yourself.

Your acknowledgement email can confirm your cost, payment terms and details if necessary.

This email should tell them how to cancel and how much notice you need for a cancellation.

Money

This chapter is all about the financial side of running an astrology business. It covers setting fees, money and value, karma, debt and tax which you can understand through your four astrological financial houses. We look at other financial indicators in your chart and the Part of Fortune.

Here we discuss your office space organization solutions. We cover burnout and making time for leisure and professional improvement. You will learn how to decide on your working hours. There is information on how to physically prepare for your clients and how to tell the world you are in business.

There are some ideas on the timing of when to quit your day job.

The Four Money Houses

There are four houses associated with money. Typically, you will use the second house as the main money house. The other money houses in a chart are the fifth, eighth and eleventh houses.

The Second House

The second house shows your earning potential. It suggests how you earn money and by what means.

This house indicates the money you may earn and for most people it is the pay you get as a salary cheque by working for others.

This house shows the credit you have available to use or in other words your credit limit. But note that once you have spent up to your credit limit it becomes an eighth house issue.

The Fifth House

The fifth house shows money you can win like the lottery. It also shows money you will put at risk like in the stock exchange or day trading and money you will gamble with which you may lose or win.

The Eighth House

The eighth house shows your debt, karmic debt, donations received and tax.

It also indicates the money you have available to you from other people (especially your partner's resources). It shows money you may receive from investments as interest, inheritances and insurance payouts.

The Eleventh house

The eleventh house shows the money you can receive from your business. Any business that you set up by yourself, like your astrology business, the income from it will be shown by the eleventh house in your chart. In the derivative house method, the eleventh house is the second from the tenth house of business. If you do not have a business, you may never use the eleventh house as a money house. Always consider the second house as the main money house in a natal chart but at times the other money houses can come into play and each situation is different.

Aspiring Astrologer Activity: Your money houses

Second House

- Find your second house cusp sign.
- Find your second ruler.
- Explore your views on earning and value in general.

Eighth House

- Your eighth house cusp sign.
- Find your eighth ruler.
- List your views on karma, debt, borrowing and taxes.

Fifth House

- Find your Fifth house cusp sign.
- Find your Fifth ruler.
- List your views on gambling, your risk appetite and the stock exchange.

Eleventh House

- Find your eleventh house cusp sign.
- Find your eleventh ruler.
- Write your views on how you see your business income and expenditure.

The Part of Fortune

The part of fortune is one of the Arabic parts or Greek lots in astrology. There are many other Arabic parts.

- Indicates good luck, grace and favour.
- Suggests ease of wealth.
- The house and sign indicate the quality of the fortune.
- Consider the planetary ruler and its condition.

The Part of Fortune and Money

The Part of Fortune has much to say about financial issues because in our society money is fortune. That is not to say that your fortune cannot come in other guises like fortunate spouses, children or friends.

That fortune is often better when it is not financially related is quite clear to many New Age travelers.

We will consider the Part of Fortune as a financial indicator in your chart.

The Condition of the Part of Fortune as Regards Money

The Part of Fortune is well placed:

- In a money house which are the second, fifth, eighth or eleventh houses.
- In Taurus or Libra which are both Venus' signs.
- Conjoined the Sun.
- Conjoined the benefics which are Venus or Jupiter.
- Trine Venus or Jupiter.
- Sextile Venus of Jupiter.
- In an angular house that is the first, fourth, seventh or tenth houses.
- Trine the ruler of the second house or to a lesser extent the other money houses.

The Part of Fortune is poorly placed:

- In a cadent house that is the third, sixth, ninth or twelfth houses.
- Square or opposite the malefic planets which are Mars or Saturn.
- Unaspected and thus it has no Ptolemaic aspect from a planet.
- Has a retrograde sign ruler.

Interpreting the Part of Fortune

The sign in which the part of fortune is placed is important and shows the nature of the fortune. The planet that rules the sign or the dispositor of the part of fortune can give more clues to the type of fortune.

Conjunctions to the Part of Fortune

Any planet conjoined your part of fortune will influence the nature of your fortune. The conjoining planet will be a powerful influence for your fortune. A conjunction to the part of fortune can sometimes overshadow the sign and the sign ruler because it is well placed.

The part of fortune is an interesting point of the astrological puzzle and a thorough understanding of the main parts of a chart are needed to understand the part of fortune. The part of fortune is one of those things that if it is not well placed it does nothing and if well placed will do much for you.

The Part of Fortune in the Houses

The part of fortune in the first house suggests your fortune comes through personal charisma and strength of your personality. Your face is your fortune

The part of fortune in the second house indicates that finances and acquisitions (art collections etc.) will be fortunate for you.

The part of fortune in the third house shows that your fortune will come through your siblings, school and learning and books, and by means of community, neighbors and local environment activities.

The part of fortune in the fourth house supports a fortunate family who may be wealthy and a good childhood environment that sets you up for life.

The part of fortune in the fifth house suggests your fortune will come through speculation perhaps on the stock exchange or lottery wins and through your children doing well in life.

The part of fortune in the sixth house indicates that your fortune will come through daily activities and your work. This placement suggests that your job can be very lucrative even if it is in a services industry.

The part of fortune in the seventh house indicates your fortune will come through partnerships and usually marriage. Your husband or wife is likely to be better off than you. Business partnerships will be of great benefit to you.

The part of fortune in the eighth house indicates your fortune will come through inheritances, insurances and annuities. You will also gain through tax (loopholes) and being scrupulous with tax affairs. You can gain through your partner's investments as well.

The part of fortune in the ninth house suggests your fortune lies in another land and that you have to travel to gain your fortune. This can be closer to home in being involved with international things and people. You can be fortunate in publishing books. You can be fortunate through the church and religion will favor you. You may be fortunate because of your philosophies in some way. You will be fortunate to have a good education.

The part of fortune in the tenth house indicates you will be fortunate in the public eye, either through your chosen career or perhaps politics. Your reputation will be good and benefit you even through challenging times. You may be fortunate to be well-known, famous and have status.

The part of fortune in the eleventh house indicates that you will be fortunate through your associations with others, either in causes or groups. You may have friends that provide support financially and are generous on your behalf. You can benefit through the people you know.

The part of fortune in the twelfth house indicates you can benefit through institutions (hospitals, libraries, prisons, zoos etc.) you can be fortunate in your private life. Your fortune is likely to be kept quiet. You may consider yourself fortunate when you give it all away and surrender (the money) to others in charitable ways. You may also squander any fortune that comes your way.

Aspiring Astrologer Activity

Note your Part of Fortune's sign.

Note you Part of Fortune's house.

List any conjunctions to your Part of Fortune.

Suggest three ways this Part of Fortune may work in your life.

How to Set Fees

The cusp of your second house, its ruler and tenants show:

- Your earning potential.
- Your attitude towards saving and spending.
- Your self-worth.
- How you value yourself.

No Free Reading

There is no free reading.

I recommended that you do not offer readings for free. It is better if you do readings for a coffee as a barter or perhaps for a $5 donation.

If you do not value your work no one else will.

What to Charge for a One Hour Astrological Consultation

The amount that you charge needs to be in line with your knowledge and experience.

If you have been studying astrology for less than three years you will charge less. If you have been studying charts for over ten years (but only look at five chart a year) you will charge less.

If you have been studying astrology for five years and see 50 to 100 charts each year you will charge more.

Take the number of charts you have read in the last twelve months and times it by the number of years you have been studying astrology.

Examples for a low price

Five charts and one year 5 x 1 = 5

Five charts and three years 5 x 3 = 15

Twenty charts and one year 20 x 1 = 20

Five charts and five years 5 x 5 = 25

Examples for a moderate price

Fifty charts and one year 50 x 1 = 50

Twenty charts and three years 20 x 3 = 60

Twenty charts and five years 20 x 5 = 100

Fifty charts and three years 50 x 3 = 150

Examples for a high price

One hundred charts in five years 100 x 5 = 500

Fifty charts and ten years 50 x 10 = 500

Everyone is different, and you need to find your sweet spot where you are being compensated for your experience and abilities.

Remember you are not the same as the next astrologer and you should price your consultations in relation to your own skills.

The amount you charge can be directly related to the minimum wage for your area. If the minimum wage in your area is $8/h use that number. If the minimum wage in your area is $13.25/hour use number.

Aspiring Astrologer Activity

How many years have you been studying astrology?

How many charts have you cast in the last twelve months?

What is the minimum wage in your geographical area?

Take the number of years, times the number of charts, times the minimum wage per hour in your area and divide it by ten.

Example:

Number of years x number of charts in the last twelve months x minimum wage / ten

1 year x 20 charts = 20 x minimum wage (say $10/h) = 200 divided by 10 = $20. So, charge $20 for a one hour consultation.

2 years x 40 charts = 80 x minimum wage (say $13/h) = 1040 divided by ten = $104. So, charge $104 for a one hour consultation.

5 years x 50 charts = 250 x minimum wage (say $14/h) = 3500 divided by 10 = $350. So, charge $350 for a one hour consultation.

Use this as a guide. Every situation is different.

How to Handle Requests for Free Readings

Astrology is a Luxury Item

To my mind professional astrology services are a luxury item. You do not need astrology. No one needs it not like bread and water. You can get free astrology anywhere online but if you want an experienced practitioner that is something else. I do give back to the astrological community and pay-it-forward, as I donate one hour of my time every month to those in need.

Why Giving a Free Reading is a No-No

If you read for others for free, you place them in a situation where they owe you a karmic debt (eighth house). This is not a good thing to do and can be avoided by making sure they see value in your work and reciprocate with something of equal value.

If you are uncomfortable charging money for your early readings, then to start with you can "charge" them something as little as a coffee. This is called bartering. It is a "token" payment acknowledging the value (second house) you place on yourself and your work.

Why are Astrologers Expected to do Work for Free?

I get it all the time.

Client, "Do not worry, I'll bring the cash to pay you for the consultation on the day and that way you and I do not have to pay PayPal fees."

Ok.

After the consultation is completed (and overrun on time), "Well, actually, I had to pay for parking downstairs, so I do not have all the money you want, and I cannot pay the full amount. But, here is what

I have in my pocket," she throws crumpled notes on the table and some coins that spin and clatter, "I'll bring the rest tomorrow."

Oh, ok.

Still waiting…

This One is a Classic

"Please come and teach your fabulous classes at our friendly venue. It is only a forty-five minute journey from your house on the bus and a ten minute walk each way. We will add thirty percent on top of your costs to our community, to cover our expenses, so do not worry."

Oh, ok.

Next day, "Um, my husband and myself want to come into the class for free, and can you cut your prices in half for the others, and can they pay in bits?" Really?

Needless to say, I cancelled the whole thing.

Some people will nickel and dime the life out of you. They cannot help it because they are coming from a place of want, a want for money and a want of not having enough.

Offering Discounts

You have a retail price to provide padding for discounts that you will offer now and then. The types of discounts may vary from business to business, but I use the following few distinct discounts:

Student Discount

For children and students, that is customers under 19 years of age, I give them less ten percent of my listed price for consultations and readings.

Seniors Discount

Seniors are people over sixty years of age. They are also known as old age pensioners (OAP) and other terms like super seniors (over seventy-five years), and bonus seniors (over fifty-five years). It is up to you. Typically, I would give seniors less ten percent of my retail price.

Seasonal Discount

During the year you have a chance to offer everyone a seasonal discount. It depends on your product and market. For instance, you can offer a Valentine's discount or a Christmas discount or a Thanksgiving discount. Typically, this would be ten percent off your retail price.

Suggested Seasonal Discounts by Month:

January - New Year discount.

February - Valentines and Chinese New Year discount.

March - Spring discount.

April - Easter discount.

May - Mother's Day discount.

June - Father's Day discount.

July - Summer sizzler discount.

August - Vacation discount.

September - Back-to-School discount.

October - Halloween discount.

November - Thanksgiving and Black Friday discount.

December - Christmas discount.

Birthday Discounts

You may consider offering a birthday discount if they book their reading or consultation and pay in their birthday month. The benefit of offering a birthday discount is that you only have to print one solar return chart and can use it for the reading.

Also, everyone with a birthday in the same month will have a similar solar return chart so it speeds up the readings for those clients who come for a reading in their birthday month.

Discounts can be used at your discretion and are in place to stimulate business in quiet times.

Early Bird Discounts

If you sell classes, workshops, conference space or eBooks you can offer an early bird rate. Those clients who book and pay before a certain date, receive the item with an early bird date. After the day the price goes up.

This encourages early sign-ups and early money in your hand. The idea is to have some discount money in reserve in your retail price. If you charge wholesale or plain cost prices, you have no room to discount your goods or services further

Discounts are good in lean times and can generate interest in your product.

Giving

I also have a system of accepting free readings in some circumstances. For instance, I offer free readings for people in wheelchairs, or otherwise disabled. I have a system and the rules are clearly stated on my website under which situations I offer free readings and which not.

If people ask for a discount or free reading I send them the link to my giving page and they have to write to me to ask for consideration for a free reading. But, the average person who has a job, and runs a car and goes to the gym can pay me the going rate.

Some people feel they should always get a deal just because, and for no particular reason, but I do not offer this type of discount.

Be prepared to have an answer when people quibble about money.

Value Propositions

Do not list your consultation fees on the web. You will be judged by your prices against others who are weaker astrologers than you.

When to Quit Your Day Job

Your day job is the one you have to go to each day. Many people have a day job and go there Monday to Friday and about forty hours a week and they get paid a salary.

Some people also have a part time job or another job on the side.

The reality is that making a full-blown salary from astrology alone is a huge challenge. You can go back to the first chapter in this book and read about professional astrologers earning over one thousand US dollars each month and master astrologers earning over five thousand US dollars a month.

Making Ends Meet

As a professional astrologer you may be able to make ends meet on one thousand dollars each month or not it depends on what your financial needs are. This need can change as your situation changes.

For example, if you are a single woman living frugally you will manage. But, if you have three kids and are a single Mom then you may not make ends meet. If your kids go to college you may have extra demands on your income and so your situation can change.

This highlights how over the course of your life your income will change. Just because you can manage on your astrology earnings today does not mean you will cope next year. By the same token if you are struggling to get enough income now from astrology alone, you may easily grow your business to cover your costs in the future.

Calculate When to Quit your Day Job

Income (money in)

Day job total net income (gross after deductions).

Plus, any other income.

Total income each month (Income).

Expenses (money out)

Income less expenses

When your income from astrology exceeds the income you get from your day job less outgoings, and you have twelve months living expenses saved in the bank, only then can you quit your day job.

Your Office Space and Working Hours

Your Work Space

If you do face-to-face consultations, you will need space in which to work. Ideally your space should be a room with a door for privacy and be cool and comfortable. You need a desk for all your papers, computers and other office goodies. Do provide refreshments. No kids, pets or other noise.

Taking a Client Appointment Booking

If you offer consultations, you will need to book the appointment with your clients. You need to send a confirmation email and have enough time (about one week) to prepare your client's charts and forecast information.

Always take a deposit.

Your Working Hours – Your Business Hours

Decide beforehand your working hours. Think about when and how often you will be available for client work. Get these times in your diary now.

Personally, I accept clients from 7am to 9pm Monday to Thursday, Friday 7am to 12 noon and not on weekends, but other times may work for you.

Aspiring Astrologer Activity: Your business hours

List the times each day that you are available for clients:

Sunday - Morning: Afternoon: Evening

Monday - Morning: Afternoon: Evening

Tuesday - Morning: Afternoon: Evening

Wednesday - Morning: Afternoon: Evening

Thursday - Morning: Afternoon: Evening

Friday - Morning: Afternoon: Evening

Saturday - Morning: Afternoon: Evening

Days you are not available for clients

Family vacation (three or four weeks each year) because you vacation for two weeks in the months of _____ and _____.

Astrology conferences, retreats and professional improvement (three to four weeks each year) because you go to astrology conferences in the months of _____ and _____.

Your Assets and Liabilities

In the world of finance there are two special words, assets and liabilities. You may have come across these terms if you have ever raised a mortgage or taken a loan from a bank. At times it can be difficult to decide whether something is an asset or a liability. There is a simple way to remember which is.

Assets feed you, and liabilities eat you.

An asset is anything that brings in money, so you can buy food. A liability is anything that you have to pay for and will eat you if you ignore it.

Examples of assets are:

- Clients who pay.
- Your day job that pays you.
- Passive income.
- Any income.
- Donations you receive from others.

Examples of liabilities are:

- The rent on your apartment or flat.
- Your mortgage - and therefore your house with a mortgage.
- Your car repayments - either hire purchase or a lease.
- Vehicle maintenance, insurance, gas (petrol) and parking costs.
- School fees for you and your kids.

- Health care costs.
- Vacation costs.
- Food and groceries.
- Personal grooming services.
- Your pet costs, food, vet and doggy hotels.
- Your kids allowance.
- Donations you make to others.
- Stuff bought on credit cards.
- Stuff bought on store cards.

Things that Seem like Assets but are Really Liabilities

Homes you Buy

We are brought up to believe that buying a house is our greatest asset. It is only an asset when it pays you. It can pay you if you took in a lodger to live in the basement, and your lodger pays you rent, that is bigger than the mortgage and property taxes on the home.

Art and Jewelry, you Buy

Investment art and jewelry costs money to buy. When the art hangs on the wall or the trinkets lie in a drawer they are not an asset because you do not get income from them to buy food.

Only on the day you sell your art and jewelry will they become an asset, as you bank the money, and buy a bucket of chicken to take home to your family.

Examples of what are not assets but seem like they are:

- A house with a mortgage.
- A car not fully paid for.
- Jewelry lying in the drawer.
- Art hanging on the walls.
- Holiday homes (unless you rent it out for profit).
- Timeshares.

Daily Time Challenges

You can make more money, but not more time, so use your time wisely. To manage time can be a challenge for many astrologers and other micro business owners who venture out on their own.

This chapter deals with how much time each chart will really take you to read and discusses the amount of hours you are prepared to spend on each astrology related activity that is not actually a chart.

It will suggest where you can adjust your life on a daily basis to find the time you need to pursue your path and ultimately live the life you want.

Your Productive Preparation Time

I am often asked by those learning astrology, "How much time do we really have to put in for each chart reading for a client?" This comes down to, how long should you spend analyzing a natal chart or a forecast before the consultation a month, a week, a day or an hour?

There is no exact answer because it depends on your level of astrological expertise and the depth of interpretation required for the client. Sometime has to be spent in prep work for each and every session.

If a consultation is booked for one hour, how many hours does an astrologer spend in preparation work before the appointment? When I first began as a professional astrologer (that is one who takes money for astrology services), I needed at least a week to plough (I mean work) through the chart. I would explore all the permutations of the astrology and cover everything I could think of. Every time I discovered a new technique I would slavishly add it in to the list things I did. There was no end.

Now, I probably spend as much time in prep as the session is in reality. So, if I have a client booked for a one hour session I will likely spend one hour analyzing the chart or charts beforehand. If it is their second or third consultation (where we are working through and exploring several themes in their lives) I try to keep it the same. One hour prep for one hour consultation. This is my plan. It can, and does, overrun but you have to draw the line somewhere. If I have a client booked in for a sequence of say, three sessions over the course of a few weeks, I will spend three or more hours preparing their interpretations. It does not matter if it is the first or the third in a sequence of consultations the prep time is the same. Of course, I can easily do more preparation work. Some charts need more, but if I am to see one or two clients a day that is what I do. Other astrologers may have different methods.

A Day in the Life of an Astrologer

They used to say, "If you want something doing give it to a busy woman." I suppose now it would be a busy person. But it seems that the more you do the more you can do. The less you do the less you want to do. After years of tweaking I have settled on a loose timetable that suits my family. I say loose because that is what it is, flexible and evolving.

Monday, Tuesday, Wednesday and Thursday

My full workday follows much the same pattern all week from Monday to Thursday. Friday and the weekend are different. I like to wake up early at around five o'clock.

5:00 – 7:00 Writing time.

7:00 – 8:00 Family breakfast.

8:00 – 10:00 Client or class preparation for that day.

10:00 – 12:00 Client consultations.

12:00 – 12:30 Lunch.

12:30 – 1:00 Walk outside in the fresh air.

1:00 – 2:00 Emails and catch-up.

2:00 – 4:00 Client consultations.

4:00 – 7:00 Family time and dinner.

7:00 – 9:00 Evening classes

If I do not have clients or classes on a particular day, then the prep and consultation time goes to writing.

I teach assorted astrology classes for four days a week. Courses are usually in the fall, winter and spring. Sometimes I offer classes in between as well if there are overflow students on the wait list. This is also the time when I do one-to-one mentorship or specialty master classes like student exam prep.

Writing means working on my client's written astrology reports, writing book manuscripts, articles, eBooks, preparing lecture notes, website blog post prep and other writing. This is creative time and not answering emails or queries which is done later in the day after lunch at 1pm.

Friday

I work until noon then I have a standing lunch date and take the rest of the day off.

Saturday

Sometimes I have an afternoon class or lecture but not every week.

Sunday

I like a slow Sunday morning. I pick up some magazines or read the astrology trade periodicals and have coffee and brunch. Maybe I will take a nap in the afternoon.

When our children were younger we had a, "No other people's kids in the house on Sunday" rule. This meant all sleepovers had to be from Friday to Saturday, so we could have Sunday in peace.

Sunday is like the twelfth house in a chart. It is a time to reflect, replenish and recharge.

7 Days to a Better Chart Reading

You Can Improve Your Astrological Interpretations in One Week.

Simply follow this seven day plan to get your readings back on track. By taking these simple steps you will be ready to present the best consultation you can muster on Saturday. That is in just six sleeps!

First you will interpret the natal chart and secondly selected forecast work. At the end you will not have considered every single little detail, but you will have looked at the important components of the natal chart and forecast indicators.

Sunday: Book and Print your Client's Charts

Book a client for next Saturday. It can be a family member, a friend or new person. But it must be a chart for someone you have not done before. Make it a one hour session.

Choose a consultation time when the transiting ascendant is in the same polarity as your Sun. If your Sun is in the passive polarity make the consultation time when a passive sign rising and the same for active signs.

Get their chart details, print out the natal chart, transits and progressions. Cast and print the consultation chart (the chart of the time and place where the consultation will happen).

Use a bi-wheel with the natal chart in the center and secondary progressions on the outside. By hand, write in the current positions of Uranus, Neptune and Pluto outside the bi-wheel.

Do not start the written interpretations yet.

Color in the major natal aspect patterns. T-Squares in red, grand trines in blue, yods in green and Thor's Hammers in orange.

Highlight the chart ruler and any sign or house emphasis in yellow.

Monday: The Balances and Strengths

Today you start writing your notes. As you write, list all the short form codes (see appendix) in the margins and explore the full interpretation meanings in the body of the page.

- Find the balances in the chart.
- Active and passive planets.
- Elements and mode strength.
- Strong signs and houses.
- Major aspect patterns.

Know the strong parts of your client's chart as these will be features they are aware of already. When they hear you discuss these issues it will make you look good and seem capable straight away.

Pull Out the Other Chart Highlights

- Most elevated planet.
- Oriental planet.
- Final dispositor etc.

Tuesday: The Ascendant and Chart Ruler

Explore the Ascendant complex.

- Look at the sign on the ascendant.
- Consider the aspects to the ascendant.
- Note any planets rising or placed in the first house.

Explore the Chart ruler complex.

That means the planet that rules the sign on the ascendant (use traditional rulers).

- Look at the chart ruler's sign.

- Consider the chart ruler's house.
- Note the chart ruler's aspects.

Write out your keywords and fully understand each and every detail. If there is an aspect you are not sure of, for instance Mars conjunct the Ascendant, research it thoroughly by reading the aspect in your cook books and on-line. Get to know that particular aspect so you will always be able to interpret it when you see it again.

Wednesday: The Luminaries

Explore the Sun complex.

- Look at the Sun's sign.
- Consider the Sun's house.
- Analyze aspects to the Sun.

Explore the Moon complex.

- Look at the Moon's sign.
- Consider Moon's house.
- Analyze aspects to the Moon

Note the Lunar phase and make sure you know what it means. Consider the lunar nodal axis by sign and house. Look out for planets squaring the nodal axis.

Thursday: Forecast for Money and Career

Explore the Midheaven.

- Note the Midheaven sign.
- Midheaven aspects.
- Planets in the tenth house.

Explore the tenth house ruler.

- Note the tenth ruler's sign.

- Note the tenth ruler's house.
- Note the tenth ruler's aspects.

Consider the transits
- Consider any transiting planets in the second house (money).
- Look for transiting planets in the sixth house (job).
- Note any transiting planets in the tenth house (career).

Look at the secondary progressions.
- Consider the second house progressed ruler.
- Look at the sixth house progressed ruler's condition.
- Explore the tenth house progressed ruler's condition.

Friday: Forecast for Love and Romance

Explore the fifth house as this is where love begins.
- Note the fifth house cusp.
- Explore the fifth house ruler by sign, house and aspects.
- List any natal fifth house planets.

Explore the seventh house of partners and spouse.
- Look at the seventh house cusp.
- Consider the seventh house ruler.
- Note any natal seventh house planets.

Explore the transits.
- Consider any transiting planets in the fifth.
- Interpret any transiting planets in the seventh.

Explore the secondary progressions.
- Check the progressed fifth house ruler's condition.

- Look at the progressed seventh house ruler's condition.

Saturday: The Consultation

Prepare yourself to give. A consultation takes something from you as an astrologer.

You need to be prepared to offer your understanding, advice, energy, time and sympathy to your client.

- Make sure the consultation room is cool and well ventilated.
- Read "10 things to do before your client arrives".
- One hour before, re-read your notes.
- Five minutes before, breathe in... breathe out...

Enjoy.

10 Things to Do Before Your Client Arrives

Ten Things to Do Today

There are ten things you can do today to make your astrological consultations easier before your next client arrives. These strategies will help you set the stage for an effective reading. I work at my family home office, but your situation may be different so find which suits you.

1. Check Your Client's Details

It has happened before, and it will happen again. If you type 1066 instead of 1966 into your software program the Sun will still be in the correct region of the zodiac but the whole chart will be out by nine hundred years! This happened to me in the early days of my client work and it is now something I always double check. There is no point in spending hours working with incorrect information.

2. Cast the Consultation Chart

I create a chart for the time of the actual consultation. It provides valuable information on the mood of the day. There are sometimes when I prefer not to see clients at all which is during the month when the Sun transits my twelfth house.

I find my time is better used in rest and recuperation to build up for the next stage when the Sun conjoins my ascendant and the solar cycle begins.

3. Your Sun's synastry

Your Sun's contacts to your client's chart will show how well you will be received by them as you illuminate their life through your solar position and the connections made by your Sun to planets in their chart. If your Sun contacts their ascendant you have the potential to influence them. If your Sun trines their Venus, your client will love what you present. If your Sun is in a hard aspect to their Pluto they may be suspicious of you, what you have to say or even astrology in general.

4. Fido is a No-no

If you own a dog it should be in another room and not seen or heard. There should not be a whiff of pooch. You do not want Spot jumping up and licking people as they walk in the door.

Having a cat about can be unnerving for some people. You may not be able to project a professional image with Whiskers sleeping on your desk.

The only animals which I believe are appropriate in a consulting room are fish in a sparkling tank.

5. Let in Fresh Air

Where I live daily winter temperatures can get down to a brisk -15C but I always open the window to my office before a client arrives because it allows fresh air in and any residue of the previous client such as lingering emotional expressions to leave. You can also burn sage and waft it about. Other astrologers I know have their own ritual cleansing techniques and I urge you to find something that you like.

6. Prepare Refreshments

Common courtesy dictates you offer some form of refreshments. For my clients I will prepare regular tea or coffee and cookies. I also let them know beforehand that they can bring a specialty tea bag if they wish. I have the tea tray ready to go and the water boiled before they arrive. I make the beverages before we sit down. Chilled iced water is placed on a table in the room before they arrive.

7. Record, Rewind and Replay

I invite my clients to bring their own recording devices. In the past I found it was too stressful when I realized, after an hour and a half, that I had forgotten to press the "record" button, and all was lost. I discovered that burning disks and making MP3's was not my strong suit. I no longer offer taping (yes it used to be called that) as part of my service but I encourage people to bring their own cell phones or recording machines, which for me, is the best solution.

8. Turn your Phone to Silent

It is not just your phone that needs to be on silent anymore, you have to make your email notifications, pings and alerts go away as well. If you have other people in your home, they need to keep it down too. Your ringing phone intrudes into your concentration and breaks your train of thought. By the same token, if your client puts their phone out and when it rings take the calls, that is down to them. It may seem rude, but it is their session after all.

9. Meditate or Ask for Guidance

Before a consultation I strive to find a calm mental place. Meditation is a good strategy. It is beneficial to be relaxed and focused and being so helps you to do your best work. People like talking about themselves and an astrology consultation is all about them. At the same time, you need to be aware of being sucked in to difficult situations and to protect yourself from being psychically drained.

10. Breathe in… Breathe out…

If you have ever been in a yoga class, you know the power of breathwork. Slow breathing calms your physical body and can lower your blood pressure. The knack is to concentrate on breathing out only, as you will naturally inhale. When working with your clients becomes stressful it shows in their experience of you, your consulting skills and ultimately astrology.

5 Things to do After your Client Leaves

1. Cleanse the Space

I do not mean sweep the floor what I do mean is open a window, burn some incense or light a fragranced candle. Clean the whiteboard and wipe the slate. Past clients leave emotional residue and it is important to purge the atmosphere and yourself from any negative emotional buildup. This practice clears your working space and helps you prepare psychologically for the next person.

2. File Charts Away

this may seem obvious, but it starts slowly, with a few files on the corner of your desk and before you know it has grown into a quivering heap of papers. Even if you only have two clients a week keep their chart notes and files neat and in a filing cabinet. You will need to refer to them later if your customer contacts you or there is a question about the reading where more clarity is needed and the following year when they come for a consultation.

3. Close out comments

I like to send a thank you note or email. It may be old fashioned, but it is a way of having closure on the session. Some clients will come back within a day or two with queries and questions and if I can remember the chart I will dash off an email spelling out the explanation. Other clients will contact me two months after the reading with questions but by this time, if I have to look at the chart again, then there will be a perusal fee.

4. Follow up Reminders

If you diarize your client's birth date you can issue consultation reminders the month before their birthday. Most astrologers offer a discount for all those with the same Sun sign as the transiting Sun.

By this method all Virgo's will receive a discount on astrology services during late August and early September every year. Having follow-up consultations near their Solar Return charts helps so you do not have to cast two.

5. Reinforce Your Weaknesses.

How did it go? Did you encounter a difficult part? Do you need to read up on a particular area of interpretation? Do you want to engage in a peer review with another astrologer? Are you exhausted, drained, elated or a combination of all three?

Complete your consultation review form. Learn from each and every reading. Do not become complacent. Stretch yourself. It is amazing what you can do.

10 Classic Comments Clients Make

Astrology is a Fascinating Subject

It draws in individuals from many walks of life. As a professional you meet numerous varied and interesting people. Perceptions that clients have of an astrologer's abilities are clearly shown in the wide range of remarks that are heard in a consulting room. These comments simply highlight the point of view held by the average person. Take a look through the list below and see if anything rings true for you.

1 "If I hadn't already paid I would have cancelled."

This is a classic comment. The client is wary and apprehensive. Had he, or she, not made the payment they would have not have arrived at the appointment. The solution may be to take a deposit at the booking. The hard truth here is, if you do not accept remuneration upfront, you will probably experience many no-shows.

2 "I have brought a friend to sit in on the reading."

This happens with brand new clients. If he or she has not already met you, they could have a vision that a consultation includes the slaughter of a chicken and writing in blood. They are apprehensive of what is to come. It may seem crazy that anyone would think this. It is your job to ensure you present a professional countenance at all times.

3 "I thought you may say I am a bad person."

This stems from the view that astrologers are in some way able to criticize or judge their customer's character, actions or lifestyle choices. We all feel we could be better in many ways and your client thinks that you can see his or her flaws and will comment about them. Everyone is acutely aware of his or her shortcomings. Perhaps you need to emanate an impression of kindness and understanding. Being an astrologer places you in a strong position over others, or so it seems to them.

4 "I was wary about what you could tell me."

They are not sure of the reach and depth that an astrology consultation can take. It is natural to be unsure of being exposed in some way. It is your job as the astrologer to make your client comfortable. Reaching out to people can take many forms. Discuss the obvious chart indicators before delving into the darker realms of their chart.

5 "I was worried you would not like me."

Often the client thinks you will make personalized comments about their life or their way of living. He or she may have old ideas carried forward over the past two thousand years when astrology was brought from the dark ages into the twenty-first century.

6 "I thought you were going to tell me I am going to die."

There is a common misconception that the general public thinks the natal chart automatically says when someone will die. Your customers generally do not want to know this type of information. Even if you believe you can predict death it is not advisable to discuss your thoughts on the matter. Probably the best way to quash their fears is to state at the booking that you will not be talking about their demise.

7 "You have the power today which concerns me."

Many people fear giving up their personal power or control and this can show up in a client's resistance to a reading. It is only natural and comes under the title of "letting others in." Astrology is tantalizing to many people. The thought that someone can see into their very being is very self-centered and which is what we offer in readings. One hour to discuss the individual and only them is intoxicating for some but daunting to others.

8 "I do not believe in astrology."

A section of people does not believe in astrology but at the same time they are curious. This is an opportunity for you, as an astrologer, to explore the chart in a way in which your client is comfortable. Focusing on the main message of the squares in a chart will give your client something to immediately relate. The best outcome for this person is that they leave the consulting room with a positive image of you, the modern astrologer.

9 "I am anxious about this."

Many people are indeed anxious about laying their soul bare to the intense scrutiny of an astrologer. Your very presence can make some individuals twitchy. We are in a counseling profession. Your customers need to feel safe. This can be achieved by allowing them to work through their issues in a supportive environment.

10 "Will you tell my wife?"

There is only one correct answer here. "No, I won't tell your wife." Whatever comes out during an appointment, the good, the bad and the ugly, remember that discretion is everything. You have to be confidential with your customer's disclosures. No doubt you will hear things you wished you had not but that goes with the territory. Astrologers who do not hold their client consultations private will soon have a reputation as such

It is up to you as an astrologer to be prepared for your client's general apprehensions and worries about astrology. Much of these misconceptions can be allayed by the professionalism that you bring to your work. The public needs to discover that modern astrology is both relevant and useful. First prize is for your clients to go forward speaking your praises and those of our profession.

Make sure you not only have excellent interpretation skills, so you can correctly delineate a chart but also ensure you bring your human side and add to astrology's reputation in a positive way.

How to Give an Astrological Referral

"Go ahead, make my day."

In one of the Dirty Harry movies Clint Eastwood famously said, "An expert knows when it's time to call in the experts." This is exactly what client referral is all about. Astrologers cannot be all things to all people. There will be those we cannot help for one reason or another. Sometimes we need to refer our clients to other experts.

An Astrological Referral

A referral is where you, the astrologer, suggests your client consults with someone else who may be an astrologer or another person in a related field. You should know the other expert to whom you are referring and ideally you will have had a working relationship with them in the past.

Reasons to Refer Your Clients

Physical distance

The prospective client is on the phone and wants a face-to-face consultation but lives miles away. A good astrologer will know the names of those working nearby and will be able to refer to them.

Not in their field of expertise

Perhaps the client wants a chart rectified and you do not offer that service. Not every astrologer does everything. Personally, I do not work on health issues or illness, but I do specialize in conception work and children's astrology. Other astrologers concentrate on health and wellness or various related fields.

The astrologer feels uncomfortable

On occasion the energies emanating from a client may not sit well with you. It may be a gut reaction, but you know you cannot connect with this person.

No time

You are fully booked for months ahead and then are off to an astrology conference for a week, after which you are going on vacation for six weeks, (well, we all can hope).

Who Can Refer and to Whom

All astrologers can, and at times should, refer their clients to other astrologers or related practitioners. If you are a new astrologer, you may not yet know who is good and you may not be confident in referring.

Ask your teacher or mentor to provide some recommendations. If you are still at a loss your local astrology group will have a list of names of neighborhood experts to offer.

For example:

- Other astrologers in the proximity.
- Specialist astrologers (e.g. Rectification and decumbiture).
- Numerologists.
- Hypnotherapists.
- Psychics and mediums.
- Others.

How to Give a Referral

Once you have decided to whom you are going to refer your client do not give the name of your referred expert to your client just yet.

Step 1

You contact the expert and ask if they will accept this client. They too may be going away or be otherwise engaged. If this person cannot see your client, you then contact the next one on your referral list and in this manner, you find someone who will help. Briefly explain the situation and let them know you will get your client to call directly and make an appointment.

Step 2

You provide your client with the email address and phone number of the chosen one and your client can personally make the arrangements to consult with your choice.

Note on Referring Clients

In my experience if you simply give your client the expert's number they may call and discover that person will not see them either. Sometimes clients can be in a fragile state and see this lack of acceptance as a form of rejection. This unfortunate situation is avoided if you confer with the one you are referring to first and make sure your client will be well received.

I bet the buzz on everyone's mind is, "Why would I send business away when it is so hard won?" That is a question for another day.

Aspiring Astrologer Activity

Do you refer your clients?

Do you have a list of possible referees?

Do you wish to be considered an expert in a particular astrological field and if so do other astrologers nearby know this?

Your Professional Improvement

Professional improvement is not just about learning more astrology, but it is a holistic approach to your business. As time goes on you will need to know more computer things and be adaptable to the future changes in the world. It is a good thing to see where you are today and to monitor your progress, so you can look back and see the developments you have made on you journey towards your astrology business.

Your Monthly Progress Checklist

As you start out as an independent practicing astrologer it makes sense to monitor your progress. It is hard to see any improvements if there is nothing to measure your efforts against. A good idea is to track your progress. One way to do this is with a quick monthly checklist. You do not want to get to December 31st and not know where you started. When looking back, last year can easily blend into the one before. Use the progress checklist and tweak the questions now and then to reflect areas you are focusing on as your interests change over the years. Do it each month and file away for later. At the end of the year as you reflect you will probably see some improvements in general business and income and even your mood.

Aspiring Astrologer Activity Monthly Progress Checklist

Year

Month

New astrology topics or ideas researched?

Workshops, classes or events attended?

New astrology techniques tried?

New astrology books read?

New astrology peers contacted?

Number of paying clients this month?

How many classes did you teach?

How many lectures did you present?

How many articles or columns did you write?

How many words of your book did you write?

How many videos or podcasts did you make?

Totally astrology related money in? $

Total astrology related money out? $

Total monthly profit? $

Did you receive any Midheaven related honors, certificates or awards?

Write one word that describes this month in astrology.

Your Annual Astrology Review

As the year ends it is a natural time to have a look back and evaluate your progress. Your life will have altered over the past twelve months.

Experience tells us how to create our future in a conscious way. You can learn from the past and through free will you may choose your future.

In the astrological world we often see the "new year" as starting on out birthday but for your astrology business, monitor and review your progress by each calendar year from January to December.

Looking Back

It is natural to have had some good times and you may have experienced a few hard moments in the past 365 days.

If you accept that what is done has gone and you cannot change the past, then what you do from today going forward is the only you can control.

Looking Forward

It is good practice to create an astrological forecast for the next year. These predictions will likely include transits, secondary progressions and other techniques.

Make sure you stand facing in the right direction when opportunity knocks next year so you do not get caught napping.

Aspiring Astrologer Activity

This Year's Review

Which transit do you feel was the most stimulating?

Which secondary progression opened you up to deeper insights?

Which house in your natal chart was invigorated the most by astrological factors?

Were there any interesting astrological tips or tricks that you learned?

Which part of astrology will you drop because it does not speak to you?

Next Year's Plan

Which is the most important self-prediction you can make for next year?

What new astrological technique will you be exploring next year?

Do you have a plan to buy a specialty book?

Will you begin a research project next year?

List any other astrology business plans for next year.

Peer Review – Is It for You?

Astrologer's Isolation

Astrology by its very nature is often practiced in isolation. You can go for months without meeting another astrologer face-to-face. As an astrologer you may have read the recommended books and taken a course or two but why not get some direct feedback on the work you are presenting to clients?

This is particularly important in your first "public" consultations. It is one thing to forecast for family and friends and another to take the big step and consult for strangers.

I believe that as astrology is not regulated (like realtors) support has to come from inside our community. That means you and me.

Defining Peer Review

Peer review is when you ask another astrologer to look over your work and provide useful feedback. It is no good for someone to say, "Oh, yes I would have interpreted it like that."

What you need are specifics.

Areas for Peer Review Consideration Can Include:

- Manual chart calculations.
- Natal chart interpretations.
- Forecasting and predictions.

Peer review is where you go to bounce interpretations, new theories or fresh techniques which you may have developed off a more experienced person.

Your Peers

Your peers are those in the astrological community whom you feel are at the same level of development as yourself. You may also consider reaching out to more advanced astrologers and teachers. However, this may become a protégé / mentor relationship. There is a good case to create study groups of like-minded people which can work very well.

Scared of Self-exposure? Ask Yourself:

- Are you an astrologer with over ten years' experience and think you do not need help?
- Do you believe it may somehow reduce your credibility within in the astrological community if you seek peer review?
- Are you scared of self-exposure?

These are all valid feelings.

The Benefits of Peer Review

Each one of us approaches chart interpretation through the lens of our own chart. I often describe this as looking through our unique stained glass window where the nuances of our own nativity will play a significant role.

To hear that your reviewer would have come to the same conclusions and interpreted the chart same way as you do is not what you need. You will benefit from listening to another's viewpoint. It lets you see your interpretations from different perspectives.

Clearly you will not agree with everything your reviewer may say and you can still go with your guts. It is all about keeping an open mind.

Who to Call

Not all astrologers offer peer review. To find someone suitable consider the options below.

- If you have or have had an astrology teacher, he or she will be your first line of approach.
- Old teachers can refer you to other's who specialize in reviewing student's work.
- The big astrology organizations may be a resource as they have contact lists of astrology practitioners.

Aspiring Astrologer Activity – Peer Review

List any people to whom you can refer your clients.

List other disciplines or professionals that you need to get on your referral list.

Name those practitioners (both astrologers and related fields professionals) you may approach and contact for referrals in the future.

Be Yourself and Be Your Sun

I have taught many students over the years and a percentage of them have gone on to become busy astrologers in their own right. But some learners still cannot get going by themselves. They linger in no man's land between hobbyist astrologer and taking their calling seriously.

Students often say to me, "I'll never be as good as you" which in itself opens up many questions.

To my mind, you should measure yourself against you, and not me, or anyone else.

Your Fate

In fact, as soon as you make the connection that it is your fate, your journey will become clearer.

Start creating you own path in your astrological life. Do not aspire to emulate other astrologers. You have one thing different to offer which is your unique perspective. This originality is shown by the planets, signs, houses and aspects in your natal chart.

You know your chart is different to everyone else's even to other astrologer's charts.

This means you have your own path to walk on your astrological journey. You have your personal destiny to fulfill. This clearly goes as far as how you use and interpret astrology and what it says to you.

Your Heroes are Your Sun

When I started to learn astrology the great astrologers of the day were almost as Gods and Goddesses to me. I knew nothing and the more I learned the more I realized I still knew nothing *in comparison to them*.

I kept going and one day something special happened. I started to form an inkling of what my message was going to be and how I wanted to put astrology out there with my individual stamp on it.

The initial ideas were not clear. They were a bit fuzzy and tended to hang about on the edges of my mind as though waiting to be invited in. Eventually I could not ignore them anymore and I consciously gave them my attention.

New fashions in astrology start with one person's ideas that become followed by many. You could be that one person who has an idea, theory or technique which becomes all the rage in astrological circles. But first, you have to live your life in line with the energies in your chart and as stated this also means doing your own thing in your astrology.

A Successful Astrologer

To Become a Professional Astrologer takes Time and Effort

If you are a dabbler and have no interest is going pro that is fine. But if you are considering stepping up your astrological business or, tuning what you have built so far into something great, here are some ideas on what you need to get in place to become a successful astrologer.

Note: I refer to her but clearly it can refer to him as well.

A Successful Astrologer…

- Works on charts regularly. She looks at new charts, interprets and forecasts every week. She does not let a month slip past without analyzing a chart. She has charts lined up ahead for interpretation.

- Has many income streams sourced from a broad output base including; client consultations, lectures, teaching, podcasts, writing horoscopes etc. She does not depend on client consultations alone for her livelihood.

- Knows how to be easy going. She is keen to work and collaborate with other astrologers in her community.

- Knows how to press herself to appeal to different clients. She is not a one trick pony.

- Markets herself well, truthfully and consistently. She is always tending her platform and knows what works for her.

- Is easily found by Google and makes sure her website, and social media accounts have current and relevant content. Her site does not have stale, six months old and out-of-date material.

- Prices her services in the correct range, that is, she charges in the sweet spot at the intersection of her ability and experience.

- Has a network of contacts who help her promote her business, she interfaces effectively and regularly with them.

- Has a focus for her work and knows her specialty inside out. She is not a Jack (or Jill) of all trades and master of none.

- Develops presentations, courses and workshops that pay her well for her time and expertise. She has lecture outlines ready when invited to speak at a conference and gets her information to the organizers promptly. She is considered one of the "easy astrologers" to work with and she is not a prima-donna.

- Knows when it is time to call in the experts. She has a list of related specialists to whom she can, and does, refer her clients if necessary.

- Knows her message, remains in her truth and stays on track within her niche. She does not try to be all things to all people.

Your Comfort Zone

I am going to guess that you probably check out your horoscope now and then. You may even consult with a couple of astrologers each year. You may dabble in astrology. You might sometimes think about taking it further to learn a bit more. The majority of people potter in astrology.

To take the next step and sign up for a class can seem too much. Because if you begin you may have to go on even if it takes you outside your comfort zone.

Your Comfort Zone

A comfort zone exists in life when you can function and run your life on autopilot. Your days are predictable, and most activities are a repeat of what has gone before. There is nothing new and certain habits have formed.

Knowing Your Routine is Easy

Your personal comfort zone may already be stretched by life's commitments like your work expectations, children demands, partner's needs, friends' activities and even your keep-fit regime.

The Final Straw

If you add one more thing it may become too much, and you understand this. It is like the straw that broke the camel's back.

One straw will not break a camel's back but if there are already ten thousand straws as the poor beast's burden then the final straw does in fact bring enough pressure to ruin it all.

You do not want to be in that situation. The way to avoid burnout is to look at the daily activities and responsibilities you currently have and reassess them.

Your Sixth House

How you spend your day is indicated by the sixth house in your chart. It is the natural house of the sign of Virgo which is ruled by Mercury. This house shows your daily activities, rituals and habits. It also suggests where you serve others, your general health, wellbeing and work.

Any planets in your sixth house will indicate the type of approach you have to manage your day. The sign on the cusp of the house and its ruler will suggest how you utilize these energies.

All transits and secondary progressions through your sixth house or that aspect sixth house tenants will hint at behavioral changes which can be developed in line with the nature of planets making the contact, transit or secondary progression.

Saturn: Time-keeper of the Zodiac

In astrology time is under the dominion of the planet Saturn. He is the time-keeper of the zodiac and the condition of your natal Saturn by sign, house and aspect will indicate how well you can manage your time.

It will suggest if you will bother to make time for what you want to achieve (here we are talking about reading or taking a course etc.).

If you want to make time for new endeavors there are two ways to find more time.

- Add hours to your day.
- Cut out things.

Add Hours to Your Day

If you want to keep all the activities you are currently doing in your day and find more time, the best way is to get up half an hour earlier.

Cut Out Things

You may be frittering away time through little things like watching too much TV. Here the best way is to turn the box on one hour later in the evening and use that precious hour for other fun things like astrology.

The irony here is that when you do find something which you start to be passionate about you will find the time usually in the ways outlined above. If you want to learn new things you make the time and readjust your life to suit.

When the Time is Right

When you are ready to learn some astrology, you can contact me at alison@starzology.com and we will explore your astrology learning needs.

You will know when the time is right.

What Type of Astrologer are You?

"Astrologer, know thyself." – Socrates.

Ancient words but as true today as the day they were penned (or is that quilled?) As an astrologer you really do need to know your own natal chart well. Why not get a blank piece of paper and try to draw your chart from memory. This shows how well you know the ins and outs of your chart. Self-knowledge is the key to understanding others. This includes the good, the bad and the ugly, warts and all.

I may not Know you Personally, but I can Hazard a Guess About You:

- You are your own person.
- You are accomplished.
- You read books.
- You have lived.
- You have laughed.
- Your journey has brought you here.
- You can do your own thing.
- You have life experience.
- You search for more.
- You choose your own path.

You owe it to yourself to be the type of astrologer that sits well with your planetary indicators. We cannot all be the same type of astrologer. Some explore their astrology through face-to-face consultations, video forecasts, supporting the astrology community via groups, writing or being the spokesman for astrology in the public eye.

In Your Astrology Life You May Want to:

Forecast and predict.

Write a Sun Sign column.

Understand your family better.

Host a blog.

Research an obscure technique.

Be a niche guru.

Curate the astrological community.

Support others.

Teach others.

Learn astrology for your own pleasure.

Write a book.

Get you name in lights.

Be rich.

Be famous.

Be on TV.

Live your life in tune with planetary cycles.

Understand yourself.

Understand others.

All of the above.

None of the above.

Your Creative Writing Time

Mercury

Writing is a creative exercise expressed through your Mercurial energies. The actual process can easily become derailed by outside distractions. Take steps to ensure your creative writing time aligns with your natal chart.

Each Angle Represent a Time in the Day

The Ascendant is dawn, the Midheaven is midday, the Descendant is sunset and the Immum Coeli in the middle of the night. Planets placed near an angle are best stimulated during the time of day indicated by the particular angle.

Mercury Rules Writing

When Mercury is in the first quadrant that is in the first, second or third house in your natal chart, you can best express its energies in the early morning before dawn.

If your Mercury in the second quadrant that is the fourth, fifth or sixth houses of your chart, writing in the evening is best for you.

When Mercury is placed in the third quadrant that is the seventh, eighth or ninth houses of your chart, it suggests your writing will flow best in the afternoon and before dusk.

Mercury in the fourth quadrant, that is the tenth, eleventh or twelfth houses of your chart, inclines you to pen your missives in the morning and finish them before lunch.

Writing and Mercury go Hand-in-Hand

You can do this planet angle relationship for other Mercury functions as well. The timing is the same and in-line with your Mercury placement time frame. You can benefit by performing

other Mercury related activities such as:
- Preparing emails.
- Making phone calls.
- Writing your blog.
- Answering questions.
- Signing papers.
- Bartering deals.
- Closing deals.
- Booking appointments.
- Making an initial approach.
- Discussing important issues.
- Having a date.
- Speaking your mind.

There are many facets to Mercury and you can improve your communications all round by doing them at the right time.

Astrological Certification, Yes or No?

"Most people can fry an egg, but they do not call themselves chefs."

Certification

Astrological certification means that you take lessons and sit a series of exams at the beginner, intermediate and advanced level of astrology. In this way you meet knowledge criteria for astrology.

No, You Do Not Need Astrological Certification

The short answer to this question is no, you do not need certification. Anyone can set up shop and call themselves an astrologer. There are no regulations as there are with realtors or psychologists.

To my mind practicing astrology is like being an artist. Whether you are doing fine art in oils, or making wooden bird houses, it is still considered art.

Many famous astrologers are self-taught. They do not get certified because they do not have to. When you have spent twenty, or thirty years, learning your art you do know what you are doing. There is a point when experience kicks in and overcomes formal training.

Astrology is not widely considered a serious field it is generally used, "For entertainment purposes only" and this sentence is recommended by legal consultants when you open your astrology business.

Yes, You Do Need Astrological Certification

The long answer is, it depends on what you want to do with your astrology.

There are two instances when I recommend taking the class and exam route:

- If astrology is a brand new subject for you (that is if you have been studying for less than twelve months). If you are learning from scratch, you have the potential in formal classes to learn all the things you need to know so you do not have gaps in your knowledge. This is a frequent occurrence when you are self-taught.

- If you want to be considered an authority in the astrology field, either by the general public, or the astrological community.

In the end I believe it is a personal choice.

How to Become a Certified Astrologer

If you are starting from scratch it will probably take twelve months for you to become somewhat proficient in chart reading and forecasting. I recommend to my students that they spend seven hours a week in astrological study to become a good astrologer. But, to become a great astrologer you need to put in fourteen hours of study this can be as reading books, research, chart practice, astrology classes, astrology conferences and workshops each week. If you live in a main city I urge you to join your local astrology group to gather a wide experience of astrological thought by attending their meetings and participating in the astrological community.

Astrological Certification Bodies

Australia:

Federation of Australian Astrologers (FAA).

Canada:

Canadian Association for Astrological Education (CAAE).

Great Britain:

Faculty of Astrological Studies London, England.

London School of Astrology (LSA).

MA, Cultural Astronomy and Astrology – University of Wales at Lampeter.

USA:

International Society Astrological Research (ISAR).

National Council for Geocosmic Research (NCGR).

American Federation of Astrologers (AFA).

Your Place in the Astrological Community

They say it takes a village to raise a child and it may take a village to create a good astrologer.

Some of you will have by now become active in your astrological community. This section has some ideas on how to reach out to others who may be in your situation and form community.

How to Create an Astrology Study Group

Humans are Group Oriented Individuals

It is natural for us to congregate together even if it means simply sitting in a coffee shop or alone at a busy bar. The nature of people is to flock together. Did I hear "baaaa!" Like-minded people often gather to discuss their favored subject, support each other, bounce ideas off each other and explore theories amongst themselves. A study group is created when several people join forces to work, read or study something of mutual interest. As I have said many times before, astrology can be an isolating interest. It makes sense to go where you are understood and (dare I say it) everyone knows your name. Perhaps you have been thinking of getting some people together to mull over charts and if so, here are some ideas to help you formulate that plan.

When to Start

Consult your chart to find the best time to begin to build your astrology group, or any group for that matter. Bear in mind the planet that signifies the subject of the groups should be prominent. In our case Uranus rules astrology and astrologers.

Here are Some Good Times to Look Out for when Creating a Group:

- Transits to your eleventh house.
- When the ruler of your eleventh house is aspected.
- During transits to your North node. In astrology the North node suggests future people who may come into your life.
- Conjunctions to your Vertex show new people entering your life.

Who to Invite

It is my belief that the people who will benefit from your group will make themselves known to you. It is natural for strong fire and air types to get together and the same for earth and water signs.

If you give it some thought, you will probably be able to come up with one or two people who live nearby and maybe interested.

Perhaps you have a busier astrologer in your area. Send them an invite. All astrologers have the same problem as in not having many others to talk to about the ins and outs of charts. This suggests why astrology conferences, retreats and seminars are so prolific and most astrology organizations are going from strength to strength.

When to Host

You may meet once a month, perhaps every third Wednesday, from 10:00am to noon or 7:00pm to 9:00pm.

If you establish a firm day and time it makes it easier for attendees to juggle their schedule and make more appearances during the year.

What to Do

Astrology book clubs

Astrology book clubs are often the first step. One new book is chosen each month and the attendees read it beforehand to arrive prepared and ready to discuss it at the meeting. You can explore the philosophies of the author compare your views on the techniques presented or even compare the "professional" book reviews found in the trade magazines.

Astrology transit groups

Astrology transit groups usually discuss the current Moon placements and any major transits or planets changing signs happening during the month. This is a good method to support general first level forecasting techniques.

Astrology interpretation groups

Astrology interpretation groups will often discuss each other's charts comparing Jupiter placements or work through one planet each meeting going over, for instance, Jupiter in all the houses and learning by hearing how other members of the groups experience their Jupiter placement. this type of get together supports natal chart analysis and better interpretation skills.

These are just some ideas for bringing your astrology cronies together in meaningful discussion.

If you feel like hosting a group similar to one of these in your home, you can benefit by offering to do all the three type of meeting suggested above.

Astrology Software

I am often asked to recommend astrology software. Students want to know which programs to buy, how much to spend, what is needed and where to get it. They want to know if they need to purchase specific astrology programs at all when many sites will cast free charts.

For those who do want to know about buying astrology software here is how I do it.

Solar Fire

Straight off let me say I use Solar Fire and have since 2002. I always keep abreast with the software and upgrade as soon as new versions are released. I do this because even though two plus two is still four, or the Sun is in the same place in version 1.0 as it is in the latest version, other features are available in the later releases.

New discovered planets like Eris, Sedna and co. have their positions. This capability may not appeal to all, but it does to me. I became a Mac believer about five years ago. If you are too then you know what I am talking about, but I kept the windows computer for Solar Fire. My PC died a few years ago and this took away my Solar Fire.

As a busy professional astrologer, it is essential that I have full astrology calculation capabilities and I had to request the kind help of a former student to print off a couple of client charts in Solar Fire which I needed immediately for clients booked in for consultations during that week.

"Oh, but you can do it all by hand!" I hear you cry, "You do not need a computer."

Well, yes, I can calculate what I needed by hand but who has the time? Come on. Really?

Anyway, I was at a decision point and I figured I had three choices:

- Buy a new Mac astrology program.
- Buy a new Windows based computer to run Solar Fire.
- Make a Windows partition on my Mac (to run Solar Fire). I chose to buy another Windows computer and in fact it is the smallest, cheapest nay lightest notebook I could find. I only run Solar Fire on it and it is not connected to the Internet yet. It is purely standalone and dedicated to Solar Fire. Luxury.

Astro Gold

During the interim period when I did not have a PC I turned to my new favorite software app Astro Gold. This is a powerful astrology app that runs on iPhone and iPad (and I believe other devices). It is written by the Solar Fire people and is incredibly powerful.

I recently used it at a Holistic Fair in my neighborhood where I gave mini astro-readings in aid of autistic children.

The joke in my home is that if the house caught fire and the family and pets escaped, what would I grab next? Well it would be the iPad with Astro Gold. I can see myself casting the chart whilst sitting under a blanket watching the firemen do their thing.

In the end buying astrology software is a personal choice. I do not have experience with other products, so I cannot comment but this is how I do it.

Add Twelve Hours and Reverse the Signs

Astrologers Can and Do make ~~Misteaks~~

As with all things practice does make perfect. An astrologer that has been practicing for more than two years should not make many errors. Hopefully there will be less and less but when learning astrology, it is amazing what errors can creep in. I will share with you a classic mistake that I was guilty of way back in the early days of my career.

Understand the Instruction

I was living in the southern hemisphere when I began to learn astrology. In a country where astrology books were few and far between. I had Parker's the Compleat Astrologer. I began casting charts by hand with log tables, ephemerides and a Table of Houses. All was well until I came to the instruction "add twelve hours and reverse the signs." I duly added twelve hours. That was simple. At this point you get the Ascendant, Midheaven and the house cusps from the Table of Houses.

…and Reverse the Signs…

This is where I made the mistakes. I flipped the zodiac so when Aries rose it was followed by Pisces then Aquarius etc. You get the picture. I did reverse the signs by making them go backwards which is what reverse means. But clearly it should have said "…and take the opposite sign…"

Only those of you who began learning astrology before the eighties will appreciate how hard it was, or how easy it was, to make errors when doing manual calculations to draw astrology charts from scratch. Just because you have the computer programs now do not think you will not make errors. The software is only as good as the person at the keyboard.

How to Have Fun at an Astrology Conference

Astrology conferences are great fun and can be the highlight in your calendar.

If you are a student, you may consider going to your first event or perhaps you are already an experienced professional and a seasoned attendee or you could be somewhere in between. Whatever your level of proficiency to attend an annual professional event can inspire you and get the juices flowing.

Simply by being present you open yourself up to appreciate new concepts, modern methods and cutting edge theories which are constantly being developed. Perhaps you will hear about a recently discovered planet, be exposed to ancient skills or come across a speaker with whom you seem to resonate and who has the missing piece of a jigsaw puzzle which you have been trying to complete.

Hearing lectures from local and international speakers can be just what you need. Astrology can be a solitary affair and you owe it to yourself to make the most of all the seminars you attend. Surviving an astrology conference takes a bit of forward thinking and planning.

Here are some ideas on how to navigate through and make event-going a rich and rewarding experience. There are thoughts on how to be the perfect guest, make the most of the opportunity and leave fired up until the following year.

Book Early

Booking your place early has two benefits. You will receive the "early bird" discount which is quite a dollar saving and by booking early you get the pleasurable anticipation of planning your conference attending strategy well ahead. It also lets the organizers know just how to gear up for the crowds.

First up Best Dressed

If the registration desk opens at 9:00am and the first lecture starts at 10:00am you should be at the conference center by at least 7:00am. Personally I like to get there the night before. Being ahead of time gives you plenty of leeway to find the car park, check into the hotel and inspect your accommodation. Any hitches in the facilities or your room features can be fixed right away.

Register at the Desk

Take your payment receipt and any other supporting documents to the conference registration desk. Make sure you receive the full lecture schedule including all the different tracks being offered. Check to see if there have been any last-minute speaker substitutions which may affect your planning strategy. This can work your benefit as they may bring an interesting person or topic in at the eleventh hour.

Decide which Talk Matters

When you receive the current lecture schedule double check that the session which you specifically wanted to hear is still on. Make sure you know where each room is situated for the talks you wish to attend. Large venues can be confusing places and you want to end up in the right workshop.

Fuel Up

Try to eat something before the first lecture. Otherwise someone can end up sitting down next to you who has to listen to you munching away through a carrot muffin, rustling paper bags and leaving a trail of crumbs behind you. We have all sat next to someone whose stomach is growling so let us hope it is not yours.

What is your Name Again?

There is a certain resistance to the wearing of name tags at conferences. It is not to help you, you know who you are, it is so other people can learn your name. When you are introduced to many people at once it becomes difficult to remember all their names. With you name clearly visible it makes you more approachable and other people can confidently address you and you in turn can speak to them.

Peeling the Onion

Hotels and conference rooms are notorious of for being either too hot or too cold. I have seen some attendees wearing the hotel's bed coverlet to combat the efficient air conditioning. The solution to this hot topic and keep your cool is layers that can be peeled off or put back on when necessary. Women can work their pashminas to great effect here.

Have your Info at Hand

Be prepared to have your contact information at your fingertips. If you meet somebody fun and interesting, you do not want to have to write your phone number or e-mail address on the back of an envelope. It does not give a good impression and lacks professionalism. Business cards are a must at these events.

Meet Like-minded People

More than anything, professional get-togethers afford you the chance to meet people, practitioners, students and researchers in your field. Be happy to make new acquaintances. If you want to engage with others do not always sit with your cronies. There will be a percentage of first-time attendees to whom you can reach out and introduce yourself. Remember how you felt the first year?

The Art of Writing

You will need a paper notebook and pen. Most conferences have a "no taping" policy. You cannot use your digital recorder at a lecture where they provide the topics for purchase afterwards. At some hotels the use of laptop computers is also not allowed during lectures.

See You Later

Conferences and training seminars are held in larger centers to facilitate attendees travel. These cities have much to offer the visitor. Tempting as it may be to rush off and see the sights, you need to focus on the workshop content. To get the best out of an astrology conference you can try to attend as many lectures and talks as possible. Tag on a couple of days at the end of the conference to enjoy the features of your host city.

Your Eleventh House

In astrology like-minded people, friends and associates are shown by your eleventh house. Before you go to the conference look at the current transits to your natal eleventh house and its ruler. They will suggest the type of experience you will have within the group dynamic. It also shows you what to emphasize at that particular conference.

You are Not Alone

Attending any astrology get-together virtually ensures that you will be listening to astro-chatter morning, noon and night and consuming horoscopes for breakfast, lunch and dinner. It is a fantastic opportunity to soak it up and let us face it, how often in your day-to-day life do you have the chance for a serious astrological conversation with those around you?

Support the Trade Room

The crystal healers, tarot card readers and booksellers are all selected carefully by the organizers to provide a varied mix and round out your total new age experience. The trade room is an important part of any conference and you would do well to consider availing yourself of their many products and services.

Speakers are People Too

Lecturers are encouraged to meet and mingle at the varied

opportunities for social gatherings over the course of the event. After enjoying a lively talk, you may be tempted to rush and gush at the speaker. Most teachers are only too pleased to answer your questions but do not like being ambushed. All the lecturer's contact details are thoughtfully printed in your info pack, be cool.

If You Please

Just because you are not at home and are in the company of people you have never met before does not make any bad manners acceptable. Be gracious. If you enjoyed the event you can say thank you to the organizers or send a note. On the other hand, if you experienced some issues, the best way of communicating your concerns is via a feedback sheet which is usually available from the registration desk. Remember to be specific.

Share the Love

When you attend a conference, you become like an employee. You are whom the event was aimed at in the first place. Seminars and conferences can only exist with the support of astrologers and other interested people. If you wish to keep these valuable resources available it is vital to attend, show your support and spread the word.

Get you Astro-mojo Back

Whether it is your first or fifteenth conference, showing up and taking part for some or the whole event is a wonderful experience. Not everyone can be there for the whole time but taking in even one day could be all you need. It is a good feeling to have some new techniques to take into your practice, fresh ideas for areas of research and your latest friend's contact details. You want to leave feeling inspired to pursue astrology further.

Pay It Forward

It makes sense to support annual astrology get-togethers too. By your presence these events can continue to grow and evolve. Enabling the organizers to offer state of the art practices, theories, and techniques with which to broaden your skills. Astrology is diverse and has many avenues to be pursued. Discover your niche interest and rekindle your passion by attending astrological conferences.

Aspiring Astrologer Activity

Name one astrology conference you would like to attend next year in your own country.

Name one astrology conference you would like to attend next year in your own continent.

Name one astrology conference you would like to attend next year in another continent.

Your Relationship with Other Astrologers

In the relatively small world of astrology we come up against each other now and then sometimes sweetly at conferences and social events and on occasion during heated public debates. Astrological practitioners are likely to know each other (in fact they should) and they probably are doing the same type of work like consultations and services, reading charts and giving insights or teaching and lecturing.

If other astrologers are chasing the same client base as you, does that make them your competition or can you do the clever thing and turn them into your collaborators?

Competitors

If you see other astrologers as your competition what can you do? How about reduce your fees to less than theirs, offer freebies or complimentary readings or some other attempt to lure their clients away – I think not.

We are not selling used cars. There is no place for grasping in the New Age community. You create your own karma by the actions you take in thought, word and deed.

Collaborators

Collaborators work together for the common good. In this case the common good is building a solid reputation for astrology within the general public. Bringing synergy into play. Becoming a collaborator is a matter of repositioning yourself to work with people similar to yourself rather than compete with them. You have your clients and they have theirs. You attract your clients and they attract theirs simply by the layout found within your and their natal charts.

I believe that people are drawn to a particular astrologer because of the synergy between them. For instance, recently I have had a seemingly endless flow of clients and students all born when the Sun was at three degrees of a particular cardinal sign. They were not born in the same year but near enough the same day. Why? Because their Sun's make a perfect sextile to my ascendant. (Probably transiting Uranus gave a push too.)

Collaborations with Other Astrologers

It follows that if you are going to collaborate with your peers that you get together with those astrologers who have a different chart to yours.

For example, if you are a strong Aries then team up with a Virgo or a Pisces. Mix up the elements.

It will stretch you too. In this way you and your collaborator can attract a variety of clients or lecture students. It also provides the public, or your attendees, with a diverse approach to similar astrology topics.

Aspiring Astrologer Activity - Your Relationship with Other Astrologers

Have you collaborated with other astrologers in the past?

How can you collaborate with other astrologers in the next year?

List any astrologer with whom you want to collaborate in the next twelve months?

Support Local Astrology

Think Global, Act Local.

A while back there was a bumper sticker that said, "Think Global, Act Local." It was in reference to pollution and what you can do about it. The idea being that you have to think about the global implications of pollution, but you can only really make changes in your local environment. Perhaps not the best correlation, but the theory is the same. As an astrologer, or an astrology student, you can think of how you would like astrology to be viewed globally (taken seriously, taught in schools, accepted in mainstream or covered by Medicare etc.) but you can really make a difference locally.

Supporting Local Astrology Means:

- To get involved with your neighborhood astrology group or chapter if you have one.
- To create a space to form a meeting in areas where there are no recognized astrology groups.
- To reach out to other astrology practitioners and making contact.
- To get to know those who can support your practice by their different skills and interests.
- To gift your time to speak or teach at an astrology get-together.
- To attend local astrology conferences and special events.
- To serve on the board of groups (if there is one).
- To support the year-end celebrations or other milestones.
- To participate.

All the above may sound like a lot of work or be of out of your comfort zone. You may feel inadequate or so new a beginner as to have nothing to offer. But that is not so, we all benefit from cross pollination of ideas and techniques.

To know others in the astrological community takes away the isolation that can plague many budding astrologers. You will find that you are not alone and to have someone to talk to about your craft is a comfort.

What to Offer Your Local Astrology Group

If you live in a city the chances are there is an established astrology group which has meetings, lectures, a newsletter and is seemingly organized. There is much that you can you offer them.

Get their start chart. Every astrology group or organization has a "Birth chart" (or an election chart as it may be known) and they will probably have this chart posted on their website. If not, the actual chart then at least the chart details with time, date and place. Look at the group's start chart and see where your natal Sun falls in their chart by house.

For instance, if your Sun is in the group's

First house – Offer to redesign their logo or give an image overhaul.

Second house – Offer to be treasurer and ensure they charge enough.

Third house – Offer to edit the e-newsletter and build community.

Fourth house – Offer to be their historian or caterer.

Fifth house – Offer to organize the annual parties and competitions.

Sixth house – Offer to serve on the board or be secretary.

Seventh house – Offer your skills as a public relations coordinator.

Eighth house – Offer to unearth new life in both speakers and events.

Ninth house – Offer to teach a class or expand their visions.

Tenth house – Offer to help promote the group and stand for president.

Eleventh house – Offer to co-ordinate with other groups & fix the website.

Twelfth house – Offer to curate the library of books and recordings etc.

Glossary of Astrological Terms

Air Sign: The three air signs are Gemini, Libra and Aquarius.

Ascendant: The ascendant is the point on the zodiac that was rising at the eastern hemisphere at the time of your birth.

Aspect: An angular connection between planets and points in a chart. Expressed in degrees and minutes.

Besieged: A planet found between the traditional malefic planets Mars and Saturn is besieged. It is under pressure and may not function well.

Cardinal sign: The cardinal signs are Aries, Cancer, Libra and Capricorn.

Celestial Equator: The celestial equator is the projected line of the Earth's equator drawn on the backdrop of the universe. Measurements are made from this."

Diurnal: Things that pertain to the day.

Earth Sign: The three earth signs are Taurus, Virgo and Capricorn.

Election Chart: An election chart is cast to find a future time to do something e.g. a wedding election.

Element: The four elements are fire, earth, air and water.

Ephemeris: A book that shows all the planets positions on any given day and other interesting facts.

Equinox: The two equinoxes occur when the Sun is at zero latitude north or south. The dates are around on March 21st and September 21st each year.

Essential Dignity: Planets have essential dignity when they are placed in signs of rulership, exaltation, fall or detriment. Also, term and face are essential dignities.

Exaltation: A planet in its sign of exaltation is considered well placed in the sign.

Fall: Planets in fall are in the signs opposite their signs of exaltation.

Fire Sign: The fire signs are Aries, Leo and Sagittarius.

Fixed signs: The fixed signs are Taurus, Leo, Scorpio and Aquarius.

Fixed Star: A star that appears not to move usually found in the constellations. Fixed stars do move but very slowly.

Gauquelin sectors: The area ten degrees before or after the ascendant or the MC.

Hemisphere: The division of a chart in half by either the ascendant/descendant axis or the MC/IC axis.

Horary: Horary astrology answers questions posed by calculating a chart for   the time they are asked.

House: A division of the chart into twelve house.

House System: A method of dividing the chart into houses, e.g. Placidus, equal house, Regiomontanus etc.

IC: Immum coeli is at the interception of the northern meridian and the ecliptic.

Ingress: When a planet enters a sign or a house.

MC: The Midheaven or medium coeli is at the interception of the southern meridian and the ecliptic.

Mode: There are three modes, cardinal, fixed and mutable.

Matutane: Means eastern.

Most elevated: The planet that is closest to the MC by longitude and can be either side of the MC.

Mundane: Astrology of world events and countries.

Mutable signs: The mutable signs are Gemini, Virgo, Sagittarius and Pisces.

Natal Chart: The birth chart.

Nativity: The natal chart.

Nocturnal: Means of the night.

Node: The Moon's node is where the Moon's path crosses the ecliptic either north or south.

Occidental: Western or of the west.

Orb: The distance allowed that aspects may be apart but still be in aspect.

Orbit: The path of a planet, moon or star.

Oriental: Eastern or of the east.

Partile: Two planets within the same degree, e.g. 15° 00' and 15° 59' are partile.

Placidus: A house system.

Plane of the ecliptic: The Sun's path.

Planet: A main body that orbits a star.

Ptolemaic: From Claudius Ptolemy.

Quadrant: One of four divisions of a chart created by the two main axes.

Retrograde Rx: The apparent backwards motion of a planet through the zodiac.

Rising: A planet that is conjunct the ascendant.

Ruler: The planet that rules a sign or house.

Satellite: Something that orbits a planet. The Moon is the Earth's satellite.

Sign: One of the twelve signs of the zodiac.

Solstice: Two days in the year when the Sun reaches its farthest distance north or south of the celestial equator this is usually on or about June 21st and December 21st every year.

Synastry: The comparison of two charts for compatibility and usually for romance.

Table of Houses: A book listing the positions of houses depending on the latitude.

Vespertane: Western or setting after the Sun.

Visible planets: The planets that can be seen with a naked eye. The Sun, Mercury, Venus, the Moon, Mars, Jupiter and Saturn.

Water Sign: The water signs are Cancer, Scorpio, and Pisces.

Zodiac sign: The twelve signs of the zodiac that lie on the Sun's path.

Short Form Codes

Astrology short form code is a method of writing in plain English short forms of astrological details.

It is not a clever idea to use astrology fonts in general correspondence sent to others as the person receiving it may not have that particular astrological font and therefore cannot read your writing.

Recommended for use in emails, text messages and written work.

Planets

SU, MO, ME, VE, MA, JU, SA, UR, NE, PL, CH, ER. (CE, VE, JN, PA)

Points

ASC, DEC, MC, IC, Vx, AVx, NN, SN, POF.

Signs

AR, TA, GE, CA, LE, VI, LI, SC, SG, CP, AQ, PI.

Houses

1st, 2nd, 3rd, 4th, 5th, 6th, 7th, 8th, 9th, 10th, 11th, 12th.

Aspects

-0-, -30-, -45-, -60-, -90-, -120-, -135-, -150-, -180-.

Hemispheres and quadrants

NH, SH, EH, WH, Q1, Q2, Q3, Q4.

Motion

Rx, D, SRx, SD.

Aspect patterns

STEL, GR TR, GR X, T-SQ, TH-HAM, YOD, KITE, MY-REC, M GR TR.

Examples of Short Form Codes

Sun in Gemini = SU GE

Moon in the fourth house = MO 4th

Venus at thirteen degrees fifty-five minutes of Taurus = VE 13TA55

Mars square Jupiter = MA-90-JU. Saturn quincunx Pluto = SA-150-PL

Chiron retrograde in Cancer = CH Rx CA

T-square Jupiter opposite Uranus both square Sun = T-SQ (JU-180-UR)-90-SU

Default Aspect Orbs

Aspect orbs for beginners

To start with use these orbs. They are the standard aspect orbs used on my courses. Astrologers debate aspect orbs as a matter of course and it is one of the constant topics for discussion (along with houses systems) when astrologers get together. Ultimately every astrologer finds the orbs that best resonate with their type of astrology, research or work. But in the meantime, …

Aspects of longitude

Conjunction 0° – orb 8°

Square 90° – orb 8°

Trine 120° – orb 8°

Opposition 180° – orb 8°

Sextile 60° – orb 4°

Semi-sextile 30° – orb 2°; Quincunx 150° – orb 2°

Semi-square 45° – orb 2°; Sesquiquadrate 135° – orb 2°

Quintile 72° – orb 2°; Bi-quintile 144° – orb 2° (not part of the courses)

Aspects of declination

Parallel – orb 1°

Contraparallel - orb 1°

Forecasting aspect orbs

For transits and secondary progressions use an orb of 1° applying and separating. As you become more experienced you can tighten this orb down to 30' coming and going.

Recommended Reading and Software

Currently these are my Go To astrology books. They are the ones I recommend you buy when you first start to build your astrology bookshelf. This is not to say these are the only books you will need but new astrologers often ask for suggested titles so here is my offering. Over time you will buy many publications. I encourage diversity in your reading as well.

For my Introduction to Astrology course:

Llewellyn's Daily Planetary Guide.

Practical Astrology by Priscilla Costello.

The Contemporary Astrologer's Handbook by Sue Tompkins.

Astrology Realized by Nadiya Shah.

For my Introduction to Natal Chart Analysis course:

The Twelve Houses by Howard Sapportas.

Astrology and the Authentic Self by Demetra George.

The Book of the Moon by Steven Forrest.

Aspects in Astrology by Sue Tompkins.

For my Introduction to Forecasting course:

Predictive Astrology – The Eagle and the Lark by Bernadette Brady.

Planets in Transit by Robert Hand.

The Art of Predictive Astrology by Carol Rushman.

Solar Arcs by Frank C Clifford.

Planets in Solar Returns by Mary Shea.

Predictive Astrology by Sakoian and Acker.

The American Ephemeris for the 20th Century: 1900 – 2000 by Neil F Michelson.

The American Ephemeris for the 21st Century: 2000 – 2050 by Neil F Michelson.

The above ephemerides are now available in one book (purple cover) from 1950 to 2050 as well.

When buying a pair of ephemerides make sure they are both either Noon or Midnight do not get one of each. I personally prefer midnight.

For my Introduction to Synastry Course:

Synastry by Rod Suskin.

Person to Person Astrology by Stephen Arroyo.

Synastry by Ronald C. Davison.

The Astrology of Human Relationships by Sakioan and Acker.

Synastry by Sasha Fenton.

Love Signs by Linda Goodman.

Planets in Composite by Robert Hand.

Recommended Astrology Cards and Tarot Cards:

The Mandala Astrological Tarot by A.T. Mann.

Astrology Reading Cards by Alison Chester-Lambert and Richard Crookes – The Findhorn Press.

Professional Astrology Software:

Solar Fire Gold (for PC).

Astro Gold (App for IPhone and iPad).

My all-time favorite astrology book is Ptolemy's Tetrabiblos. I have an old 1822 copy which I bought from eBay years ago. I probably need to get a newer version to save this one. It has some olde worlde wording which is part of its charm. For example, Chapter 11 begins with:

"The Conception, and the Parturition, or Birth; by which latter Event quits the Womb and assumes another State of Existence."

Thank You

Thank you for reading this book. If you want more information about something you read here, or you would like an astrology reading please contact me at starzology.com and I will help you.

If you enjoyed this book, please consider giving me a positive review on Amazon.

On the other hand, if you found an error or typo (and yes, I am only human) please email me so I can fix it.

Have a prosperous day,

Alison

More for You

About the Author

Alison Price is a writer, astrologer and creative.

Alison has a diploma from the South African College for Astrological Studies, Johannesburg and a Certificate from the Faculty of Astrological Studies, London, England.

Astrology

Alison has a vibrant astrology business based in downtown Vancouver, Canada. Where she offers (in-person and through Skype) personal consultations, teaches astrology classes to a select group of engaged students, lectures (locally and internationally) and writes.

Writing

She has contributed feature articles to community astrology newsletters and has her work published in Wellbeing Astrology, Dell Horoscope and the Astrological Journal.

Alison is the editor of *Ideas* the quarterly newsletter for the Canadian Association of Astrological Education.

Alison syndicates her weekly, monthly and annual horoscopes. She ghostwrites popular new age horoscope columns. She writes for other astrologers on the new age topics of astrology, horoscopes, crystals, color therapy, symbology, Reiki, dream analysis and numerology for sites that you probably know and love.

Contact details

Website: www.starzology.com

Other Books by Alison Price

Introduction to Astrology – Beginner's

A beginner's foundational astrology book. Helps you build your astrology knowledge and you can work at your own pace.

Introduction to Natal Chart Analysis – Intermediate

An intermediate astrology book. Build your astrology natal chart reading knowledge.

Introduction to Astrological Forecasting – Advanced

An advanced astrology book. It covers the forecast methods of transits, solar returns, secondary progressions and solar arc directions.

Your Money Planets – Astrology for your financial life

This book is a guide for a positive approach to your financial life with the help of astrology. It will show you how a little astrological knowledge can make your life better. It shows you how to work with the planets for your financial benefit.

Children's Charts – Astrology for little darlings

Learn how to read a child's chart and what to look for. Explore the first few years as the child develops through astrology. Discover the dynamics of early school life and the astrological pointers that can help you and your child.

31 Days to a Better Chart Reading

This is a guide for anyone who wants to read a chart and needs to get going fast. Each day you can learn a new feature about chart reading and get better quickly. Stop fiddling about with the inconsequential and get to the meat as soon as possible. This book is the culmination and distillation of all Alison's other works on astrology learning to read charts combined in a curated whole. It contains fresh content and will appeal to a broad audience of aspiring astrologers.

Join our Community

We invite you to join our email list and receive general astrology news from Starzology, monthly advanced astrology information and other bonus goodies.

Printed in Great Britain
by Amazon